The Ketogenic Diet Cookbook

Your 15-Day Plan to Lose Weight, Balance

Hormones, Health, and Beauty

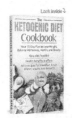

Knowledge Lab ZZ

Great World Press

V1/04

Disclaimer Notice:

Please note the information contained within this document is for educational and entertainment purposes only. All effort has been executed to present accurate, up to date, reliable, complete information. No warranties of any kind are declared or implied. Readers acknowledge that the author is not engaged in the rendering of legal, financial, medical or professional advice. The content within this book has been derived from various sources. Please consult a licensed professional before attempting any techniques outlined in this book.

By reading this document, the reader agrees that under no circumstances is the author responsible for any losses, direct or indirect, that are incurred as a result of the use of the information contained within this document, including, but not limited to, errors, omissions, or inaccuracies.

Table of Contents

Introduction

For the longest time, we have wrongly demonized dietary fats and blamed them for various health problems and weight gain. It is a popular myth that fats are undesirable and harmful for your well-being. But the fact is a diet rich in naturally healthy fatty foods helps your body burn fat and not gain weight. This is the idea the ketogenic diet is based on. Once your body starts obtaining calories from natural dietary fats, while reducing carbs, it starts burning fats for fuel. It, in turn, enables weight loss while making you feel more energetic and stronger without feeling hungry.

When it comes to a ketogenic diet, you can forget about a one-size-fits-all approach. It is easily customizable, and you can opt for a variation of the keto diet that fits your lifestyle requirements.

In this book, you'll find all the tools required for developing a personalized keto regime, which will enable you to lose weight, balance your hormones, and enhance your overall health. You will learn about the keto diet, different variations of this diet, the benefits it offers, a food list, tips to get started, and tips to build muscle on the ketogenic diet. Apart from that, you'll find plenty of keto-friendly recipes. All the recipes given in this book are divided into various categories to make it convenient for the reader. You will also find a sample meal plan you can follow while getting started with this diet.

So, are you ready to turn your life around? Do you want to lead a healthier life? Are you interested in attaining your weight loss objectives? If yes, then let us get started and learn more about the keto diet immediately.

Chapter One: Ketogenic Diet

About the Keto Diet

The ketogenic diet or the keto diet, as it is popularly known, is a simple eating pattern that primarily focuses on foods rich in healthy fats. While following this diet, a majority of your daily calories will be in the form of fatty foods. When this is combined with adequate consumption of protein and little or no carbs, it helps improve your overall health.

KETO DIET FOOD PYRAMID

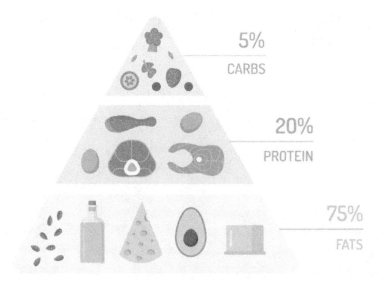

5%
CARBS

20%
PROTEIN

75%
FATS

Whenever you consume any carbs, your body immediately gets to work and starts converting them into glucose. Only a portion of this glucose is readily used while the remainder is stored for future use as fatty cells. Over a period, the accumulation of these fat deposits leads to weight gain. So, if you keep consuming more and more carbs, your body never uses any of its fat reserves. The keto diet helps reverse this process.

When you start depleting your body of its usual source of glucose, it is forced to unlock its internal reserves of fat to provide energy. So, your body essentially starts breaking down fat cells to provide energy. This process is known as ketosis, and in this stage, your body produces energy molecules known as ketones. It is where the ketogenic diet gets its name. When your body starts burning fats, it leads to weight loss and several other health benefits that you will learn more about in subsequent chapters.

Types of Keto Diet

There are three popular variations of the ketogenic diet, and they are as follows.

Classic Keto Diet

The classic ketogenic diet is also known as the standard ketogenic diet. In this pattern of eating, the ratio of macronutrient intake will be 75% fats, 15 to 20% in the form of proteins, and 5 to 10% in the form of carbs. While following this ketogenic protocol, your ideal intake of naturally fatty foods must be about 150 grams. Unless you do this, your body will never start burning fats as its primary source of energy. Simultaneously, you must reduce your carb intake and restrict it to not more than 50 grams per day. Your intake of proteins must be around 90 grams daily.

Targeted Ketogenic Diet

The targeted ketogenic diet is perfect for athletes or other individuals who lead active lifestyles. It is perfect for all those who require more carbs than the one suggested by the classic keto diet. The ratio of macronutrient intake will be 65 to 70% fats, 20% protein, and 10 to 15% carbs. If you are interested in performing high-intensity exercises and enhance your recovery process, this diet makes additional allocations of about 20 to 30 grams of carbs. These carbs must be consumed before and after a strenuous workout. When you immediately consume carbs before and after working out, your body does not store them, and instead, starts burning them to fuel your recovery.

Cyclic Ketogenic Diet

The cyclic ketogenic diet gives you an option to shift in and out of ketosis. It essentially provides a simple approach to ketosis without severely restricting your daily carb intake.

You can indulge in a couple of cheat days while following this diet without throwing your body out of ketosis. While following this diet, your regular intake of macronutrients will be the same as that on the standard keto diet. The ratio of macros you must stick to is 75% fats, 15 to 20% proteins, and about 5 to 10% carbs. However, on the off days, you can consume 50% carbs and 25% protein. A simple approach of this diet involves following the regular keto diet for five days and sticking to the non-keto diet for the other two days a week.

Chapter Two: Ketogenic Diet and Your Health

Benefits of the Keto Diet

In this section, let us look at some of the health benefits of the keto diet.

Weight Loss

Keto diet helps improve your metabolism while reducing your appetite. It also consists of certain foods that leave your tummy feeling full for longer and reduce the production of hunger-stimulating hormones. A combination of these factors assists in weight loss. You can attain these benefits without counting calories or severely restricting your food intake. As long as you stick to the simple protocols of the ketogenic diet, weight loss occurs naturally.

In ketosis, your body starts utilizing its internal reserves of fats to provide energy. So, it is not just weight loss but fat loss as well. You will essentially be consuming fats to enable your body to burn all the fats stored within.

Reduces the Risk of Certain Cancers

Researchers examined the effects of the ketogenic diet, and it is believed it can help prevent or treat certain types of cancers. In a study, it was noticed that the keto diet could be used as a complementary treatment along with radiation therapy and chemotherapy to treat certain types of cancers. A more recent study conducted in 2018 supports the previous notion because the keto diet regulates the levels of blood sugar and reduces the risk of any insulin complications. Some research shows the keto diet might benefit cancer treatment, but the studies aren't conclusive. Further research is required in this field.

Regulates Blood Sugar and Insulin

Any carbs you consume are effectively turned into glucose, a form of simple sugars. To regulate the levels of high blood sugar in the body, insulin is generated by the pancreas. Insulin enables the cells to utilize this glucose and store the rest for use in the future. A low carb diet like the ketogenic diet can be used for treating type 2 diabetes. By reducing the intake of carbs, your body's natural requirement for insulin reduces. It, in turn, reduces the levels of blood sugar.

Tackles Acne

Fluctuations in levels of blood sugar and a poor diet are amongst the leading causes of acne. A diet rich in processed and refined carbs alters the health of gut bacteria and causes significant fluctuations in levels of blood sugar. These two factors harm the skin's health. A 2012 study shows ketogenic diet can reduce symptoms of acne by reducing an individual's intake of carbohydrates.

Better Brain Health

A 2019 review suggests ketones produced during ketosis offer neuroprotective benefits. It essentially helps strengthen and protect your brain, along with all the nerve cells present within. It is one of the reasons why this diet can be used to manage or prevent chronic illnesses like Alzheimer's. However, plenty of research is required before understanding the true effect of the ketogenic diet on the brain's health. It is also believed ketosis helps reduce seizures in all those with epilepsy. It is used in combination with certain medications and drugs to treat epilepsy.

Improves Heart Health

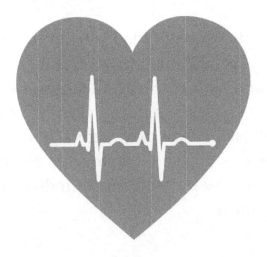

The ketogenic diet helps regulate levels of blood sugar while reducing the levels of blood pressure. A low-carb and a high fat diet like keto reduces the level of triglycerides and cholesterol in the body. It essentially increases the levels of desirable cholesterol or HDL (high-density lipoprotein) while reducing the levels of undesirable cholesterol or LDL (low-density lipoprotein). High levels of HDL are directly related to a low risk of cardiovascular diseases.

High Energy Levels

On a regular diet, your energy tends to fluctuate, especially late in the afternoon. Usually, this is when your craving for caffeine increases. While following the keto diet, you will feel fuller for longer and more energetic as well. Once your body starts consistently burning fats, it no longer depends on glucose to provide energy. Since your body no longer depends on external sources of energy to fuel itself, your energy levels will be stabilized.

Reduction of Harmful Fats

The fats accumulated between your organs are known as visceral fats, and they are extremely harmful. These harmful fatty deposits are commonly found in the abdominal cavity. Visceral fats can quickly prevent your organs from functioning optimally while increasing inflammation. It also increases your body's resistance to insulin. The accumulation of these harmful fats can be reduced drastically by reducing your intake of carbs. It, in turn, reduces the risk of certain cardiovascular diseases too.

Treating Gastrointestinal Problems

Digestive troubles like acid reflux, inflammation, heartburn, bloating, gallstones, and irritable bowel syndrome can lead to chronic illnesses when left unchecked. A ketogenic diet helps reverse all these troublesome conditions. Carbs and sugars are among the leading foods that irritate the gut microbiome and disrupt their usual functions. By eliminating these undesirable products from your diet, you can improve your overall health.

Research and Opinions

The ketogenic diet offers plenty of health benefits, but there are certain side effects associated with it as well. Most of the side effects are in the form of the keto flu. The common symptoms of the keto flu include nausea, lethargy, fatigue, and gastrointestinal distress. The keto flu occurs when your body is getting accustomed to the ketogenic diet. Once your transition into ketosis is complete, the symptoms associated with the keto flu will fade away. Fatigue is a common symptom and is caused when your body runs out of glucose for producing energy and has to start using fats. This simple transition can make your body feel tired for a couple of days. However, the effects of this flu can be reduced by drinking plenty of water, electrolytes, and getting sufficient sleep.

Anyone with type 1 or type 2 diabetes must consult a doctor before following the ketogenic diet. It usually is quite helpful for all those individuals who have hyperglycemia. However, if you're not mindful of your blood sugar levels and don't check your glucose levels a couple of times daily, it increases the risk of ketoacidosis. Ketoacidosis occurs whenever the levels of ketones increase.

Ketones are acids produced whenever your body burns fats, and when left unchecked, they increase the acid concentration in your blood. When the blood becomes extremely acidic, it harms the function of your kidneys, liver, and brain. When left unchecked, it can prove fatal. A couple of symptoms you must watch out for are bad breath, difficulty in breathing, frequent urination, extreme nausea, and a dry mouth. Seek medical help if you notice any of the symptoms of ketoacidosis.

The keto diet recommends a high intake of naturally fatty foods. However, the kind of fats you consume matters a lot. Consuming foods rich in omega-6 fatty acids and trans fats will worsen your overall health and prove to be counterproductive. Apart from this, be mindful of your intake of dietary fiber too. As long as you stick to the keto food list discussed in the next chapter, your body will get all the nutrients it requires. When in doubt, consult your doctor before starting this diet.

The keto diet is extremely helpful and will improve your overall health. With a little care and caution, all the side effects associated with this diet can be easily tackled.

Chapter Three: Food List

Meats and Proteins

While following any variations of the keto diet, proteins must account for about 15 to 25% of your daily calorie intake. Try to opt for grass-fed and organic meats and proteins instead of the factory-farmed variants. The different types of proteins you can include are as follows.

- Beef- ribs, steaks, ground beef, and more
- Pork- ground pork, pork chops, bacon (unprocessed), ham (unglazed)
- Chicken
- Salmon, tuna, sardines, mahi-mahi, and other fatty fish
- Shrimp, lobster, crabs, clams, and other crustaceans
- Eggs
- Tempeh
- Spirulina
- Tofu

- Natto
- Nutritional yeast

Note: Avoid deli meats and processed meats since they have added sugars and carbs. Carefully read through the list of ingredients before buying any processed meats like sausages, hot dogs, salami, pepperoni, or prosciutto.

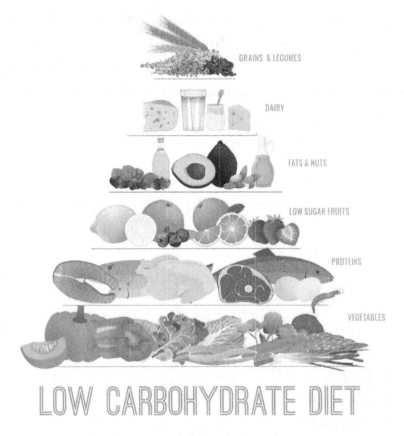

Vegetables

While following the keto diet, you must drastically cut down on your intake of starchy vegetables, especially root vegetables. The majority of the vegetables grown aboveground are ideal for the keto diet. Some of the healthy examples of non-starchy vegetables include the following but aren't restricted to this list.

- Asparagus
- Arugula
- Artichokes
- Brussels sprouts
- Broccoli
- Cauliflower
- Cabbage
- Cucumber
- Eggplant
- Green beans
- Fennel
- Pumpkin
- Zucchini
- Radish
- Spaghetti squash
- Celery

- Bamboo shoots
- Nori
- Okra
- Sugar snap peas
- Water chestnuts
- Beansprouts
- Kale
- Spinach
- Amaranth
- Swiss chard
- Bok choy
- Pak Choy
- Bell peppers and other peppers
- Watercress
- Mushrooms
- Tomatoes and olives (a fruit too)

Fruits

Avoid high carb foods like grapes, bananas, mangoes, and other tropical fruits. Sweet melons, such as cantaloupe, watermelon, and honeydew melon, can be consumed in limited amounts.

Here is a list of certain fruits you can consume on the keto diet (not an exhaustive list).

- Avocados
- Strawberries
- Blackberries
- Raspberries
- Blueberries
- Mulberries
- Cranberries
- Cherries
- Cantaloupes
- Lemons
- Limes
- Coconuts
- Tomatoes

Fats and Oils

At least 65% of your daily calorie intake will be in the form of fatty foods. Most of the facts will be from natural sources like nuts, meats, and avocados. Saturated and monounsaturated fats, especially the grass-fed sources, must be included in the keto diet.

The different sources of fats and oils you can include are as follows.

- Lard
- Unprocessed animal fats
- Fatty fish, such as salmon, trout, or sardines
- Avocados
- Egg yolks
- Brazil nuts
- Grass-fed butter
- Macadamia nuts
- Coconut butter
- Ghee
- Cocoa butter
- Extra virgin olive oil
- Coconut oil
- Mayonnaise
- Avocado oil
- MCT oil
- Macadamia oil

Note: Stay away from polyunsaturated, processed fats, and trans fats, such as hydrogenated oils and margarine.

Dairy Products

The different dairy products you can add to your diet are as follows.

- Butter
- Cream
- Hard and soft cheeses
- Milk
- Cream cheese
- Feta
- Greek yogurt
- Ghee
- Sour cream
- Unsweetened heavy whipping cream

Note: Always opt for full-fat dairy products instead of low-fat, low-cal, zero-fat, or diet options. They usually contain added sugars that will do your body no good on the keto diet.

Nuts and Seeds

When consumed in moderation, nuts and seeds are extremely good sources of healthy fats and several other nutrients. The different nuts and seeds you can include are as follows.

- Almonds
- Pecans
- Walnuts
- Brazil nuts
- Hazelnuts
- Pine nuts
- Macadamia nuts
- Sunflower seeds
- Pumpkin seeds
- Sesame seeds
- Hemp seeds
- Flaxseeds

Note: Avoid peanuts since they are legumes and aren't keto-friendly.

Drinks and Beverages

Keep it as simple as possible when it comes to different beverages and drinks you consume. Drink plenty of water to keep your body thoroughly hydrated. Stay away from processed and packaged drinks, even fruit juices, since they have hidden carbs and sugars. Black coffee, herbal teas, and water are the best beverages for this diet. Avoid adding milk or sugar (including honey) to coffee and teas you consume.

Note: Avoid alcohol if weight loss is your priority. If you do want to consume alcohol, opt for hard and clear liquors. An occasional glass of dry red wine will not harm you. Some low carb alcohols you can consume in moderation include vodka, gin, tequila, rum, champagne, pinot noir, cabernet sauvignon, pinot blanc, chardonnay, and prosecco.

Sweeteners

Curbing your urge to binge on sweet foods is a major obstacle you must overcome while following this diet. Luckily, there are a couple of sweeteners that can be consumed on a keto diet, but in moderation. Avoid sweeteners as much as you can, and if you cannot, then opt for the following.

- Stevia
- Xylitol
- Allulose
- Erythritol

Foods to Avoid

All sorts of processed and packaged foods, including junk food, must be avoided on the keto diet. Apart from it, there are certain high carb foods you must avoid like bread, pasta, rice, potatoes, corn, candies, chocolates, ice creams, chips, biscuits, sweet potatoes, and other white starches.

Chapter Four: Build Muscle Mass

It is a popular misconception that carbs are quintessential for building muscles. You can build and develop muscles while following a low-carb diet like the keto diet. A strength training regime, coupled with the keto diet, increases the composition of lean muscle. During the initial stages of ketosis, until your body gets accustomed to shifting its primary source of energy from glucose to fats, you might notice a slight dip in energy levels. Once your body is acclimatized to the keto diet, your energy levels will be stabilized, and you will feel more energetic than ever before. The mitochondrial density increases when your body is fully keto-adapted, which allows you to train quicker and for prolonged periods. Your body starts effectively and efficiently synthesizing ATP (Adenosine Triphosphate) from dietary fats and internal fat reserves to fuel even strenuous workouts.

Consumption of excess protein can end ketosis because it leads to gluconeogenesis. During this process, all the excess protein is turned into glucose, which prevents your body from burning fats. Protein in moderation is important for the efficient functioning of your body and its metabolism.

Depending upon your usual level of activity, your protein intake must vary. Here are some general guidelines you can stick to while following the keto diet.

For heavy and moderate exercise, your body requires about 1.6 grams and 1.3 grams of protein per kilogram of your bodyweight. For a sedentary or light exercise routine, your body requires anywhere between 0.8 to 1 gram of protein per kilogram of your bodyweight.

If muscle growth is your priority, consume at least 150 to 500 more calories than your usual calorie intake. Add one gram of protein for every pound of your lean body mass and consume plenty of healthy fats. Consuming more calories than your calorie expenditure leads to keto gains. A calorie surplus combined with adequate consumption of proteins helps build and develop muscles. If you are following a targeted ketogenic diet, consume about 20 to 50 grams of carbs before or after a high-intensity training session. It allows your body to quickly replenish its depleted reserves of glucose while speeding up muscle recovery.

Your body requires plenty of electrolytes to refuel itself after workouts. Monitoring your electrolyte consumption is quintessential for optimizing your athletic performance. The primary electrolytes you must monitor are magnesium, sodium, and potassium. The best sources of magnesium include dark chocolate, spinach, cashews, avocados, and almonds. Potassium-rich foods include cucumbers, spinach, broccoli, salmon, and mushrooms. A drastic reduction in sodium intake is a major mistake a lot of people make on a low-carb diet. Keto diet is diuretic, and when left unchecked, it can quickly deplete your body's sodium levels. Sodium is important for maintaining healthy muscles, so increase your sodium intake, especially before exercising. Your average intake of sodium must be between 5,000 and 7,000 mg. Before exercising, consume 1,000 to 2,000 mg of sodium to improve your overall performance.

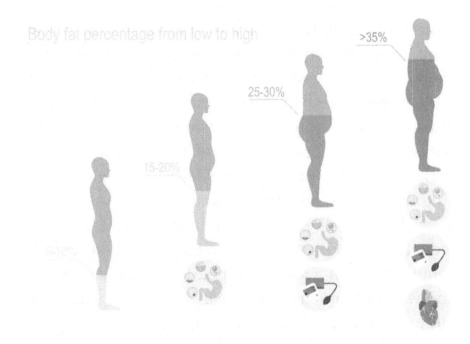

Body fat percentage from low to high

15-20%

25-30%

>35%

Here are some general tips you can use for building muscle on the ketogenic diet.

Start by Reducing Your Carb Intake

Not more than 15 to 20% of your daily calories must be in the form of carbs. You can use a carb calculator to track your carb intake. Consume sufficient protein, but don't go overboard. To build muscle, opt for strength training, and enjoy the keto gains.

You can opt for pull-ups, squats, deadlifts, bench press, bodyweight exercises, sprinting, or even yoga.

Replenish Glycogen

Glycogen is your internal reserves of glucose stored in muscle cells. Whenever you exercise, the glycogen reserves are immediately depleted. Therefore, it is quintessential that you replenish these reserves to ensure optimal performance and maintain muscle mass. Creatine is an important supplement that enables your body to synthesize and maintain its glycogen reserves. Add a creatine supplement only after consulting your doctor and once your body is used to the keto diet. Creatine helps build muscle, overall strength, prevent muscle loss, improve metabolism, and improve your cognitive performance.

Avoid Training Intensively Whenever You Fast

If your body doesn't have sufficient energy to fuel your high-intensity workouts, it starts breaking down muscle to supplement its energy reserves. If you are trying to build muscle, then avoid fasting and training simultaneously. Indulging in an occasional cheat day is fine. However, avoid indulging in constant cheat days since it proves counterintuitive. All the benefits of the ketogenic diet will become redundant if your carbohydrate and sugar intakes are high. Ketones are your primary source of energy, but don't focus only on ketones. If your body produces more ketones than it utilizes, it leads to ketoacidosis. Ketoacidosis can prove fatal when left unchecked. So, regularly monitor your ketone levels using Ketostix, conducting blood tests, or even a simple breath test (keto breath analyzer).

Body Fat Percentage

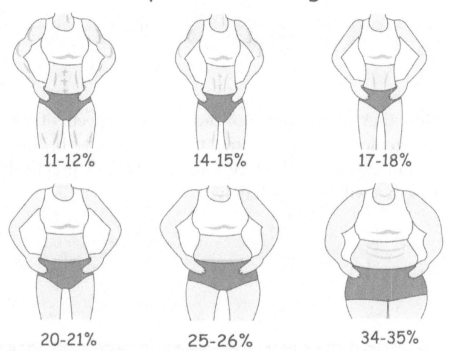

11-12%   14-15%   17-18%

20-21%   25-26%   34-35%

Chapter Five: How to Get Started on the Keto Diet

Now that you're aware of the various aspects of the ketogenic diet, it is time to get started. In this section, let us look at certain helpful and practical tips that will come in handy.

Healthy Fats

While reducing your carb intake, ensure that you consume sufficient healthy fats. If you simultaneously deprive your body of two important macronutrients- carbs and fats, you will merely be starving yourself. Ketosis doesn't occur until your intake of healthy and natural fats doesn't increase. Follow the food list discussed in the previous chapter to ensure that your body gets its daily dose of macros. Stop fearing fats and avoid skimping on fats.

Reduce Carbs

If your usual diet is rich in carbs, then your body will take a while longer to get used to the ketogenic diet. To make this transition easier, start by limiting your carb intake while increasing the intake of non-starchy vegetables. Make it a point to add at least a portion of vegetables to all the meals you consume. Most of your daily carbs will be in the form of non-starchy vegetables, such as leafy greens, so load upon them.

Support System

A dietary change might not seem like much to you, but it is a major change for your body. Talk to your loved ones about the diet you wish to follow along with your reasons for doing the same. Having your support system in place is quintessential before you start dieting. If you want, you can find a dieting buddy for yourself and get started. There are various online forums and chat groups you can join to meet other like minded people. There will be days when your motivation levels take a nosedive, and you might not want to follow the diet. On such days, your support system will give you the strength required to keep going.

Add Exercise

To efficiently speed up the weight loss process and amp up the benefits offered by the keto diet, then you need to start exercising. Include some form of exercise in your daily routine.

Even exercising three times per week will be helpful. Exercise is not just a stress buster but improves your body's metabolism along with overall health. Carb restriction and exercise are the two ways in which you can trigger ketosis easily. While exercising, stick to low-intensity workouts until your body is fully keto-adapted. High-intensity exercises during the transitioning period will harm your overall progress.

Do Your Research

Before you start the diet, consult your medical practitioner. If you have any pre-existing health conditions, then get a clearance certificate from the doctor. Apart from this, gather all the required supplies for the diet. Go through the different recipes along with the food list given in this book and come up with a grocery list. Use the sample diet plan given in this book to prepare your meals. While dieting, you must include a variety of foods, or else it will get boring. Avoid excessive repetition of the menu and do your research.

Pick a Date

Before you start dieting, ensure that you are aware of your health or fitness goals. The goals you establish will give you the inner motivation required to stick to the diet. If you have no goals in mind, then it is highly unlikely you will stick to the diet in the future. Therefore, carefully consider your goals or objectives. Starting a new diet does take some preparation.

Prepare yourself mentally for the dietary changes you will be making. You can slowly ease yourself into the keto diet and don't have to jump headfirst into it. So, select a date on which you wish to start this diet and stick to it.

Clear Your Pantry

Before you start dieting, ensure that you get rid of all non-keto foods. Think of it as essential spring-cleaning for your kitchen and pantry. "Out of sight, out of mind" is a great idea when it comes to limiting or removing temptations. The urge to binge on unhealthy foods will lessen when they don't constantly surround you.

Social Life

Regardless of what you do, don't compromise on your social life because of your diet. If you do this, it will merely make you feel frustrated and give up on a diet.

Most restaurants and food joints offer keto-friendly options these days. Make healthy and mindful choices, and you can eat out.

By following these simple tips, it will become easier to get started with the keto diet.

Chapter Six: Ketogenic Breakfast Recipes

1. Breakfast Sandwich

Cooking time: 12 – 15 minutes

Number of servings: 2

Nutritional values per serving:

- Calories – 603
- Fat – 54 g
- Total Carbohydrate – 7 g
- Digestible carbohydrate – 4 g
- Edible fibers – 3 g
- Protein – 22 g

Ingredients:

- 4 sausage patties
- 2 tablespoons cream cheese
- ½ medium avocado, peeled, pitted, sliced
- Salt to taste

- Pepper to taste
- 2 eggs, beaten
- ¼ cup grated sharp cheddar cheese
- 1 teaspoon sriracha sauce or to taste

Directions:

1. Place a skillet over medium flame. Cook the sausage patties in the skillet as per the directions on the package.
2. Add cream cheese and cheddar cheese into a microwave safe bowl. Microwave on high for about 30 seconds or until it melts.
3. Whisk well. Add sriracha and whisk until well combined.
4. Add salt and pepper to the bowl of eggs and whisk well.
5. Heat the same skillet over medium flame and add the beaten egg. When the omelet is cooked on one side, flip sides and cook the other side.
6. Remove the omelet and cut it into 2 halves.
7. Spread the cheese mixture on the omelet halves. Fold each omelet in half.
8. Place an omelet half on 2 sausage patties. Cover with remaining sausage patties to complete the sandwich.
9. Serve.

2. Brussels Sprouts Casserole Au Gratin with Bacon

Cooking time: 45 minutes

Number of servings: 5

Nutritional values per serving:

- Calories – 196
- Fat – 15 g
- Total Carbohydrate – 8 g
- Digestible carbohydrate – 5 g
- Edible fibers – 3 g
- Protein – 8 g

Ingredients:

- 1 pound Brussels sprouts, halved
- ½ teaspoon salt or to taste, divided
- ¼ cup almond milk, unsweetened
- 1 tablespoon butter
- 2 tablespoons bacon bits
- ½ tablespoon olive oil
- ¼ teaspoon pepper
- ¼ cup heavy cream

- ¾ cup cheddar cheese, divided

Directions:

1. Place Brussels sprouts in a large baking dish (9 x 13 inches) lined with foil. Drizzle oil and toss well. Sprinkle ¼ teaspoon salt and 1/8 teaspoon pepper over the Brussels sprouts. Toss well. Spread the Brussels sprouts evenly in the baking dish. Place the baking dish in a preheated oven.
2. Roast at 400° F for about 30 – 40 minutes or until brown around the edges. Turn the Brussels sprouts half way through roasting.
3. Add butter into a saucepan and melt over medium flame. Stir in the almond milk and cream and stir.
4. When the mixture is hot, add ½ cup cheddar cheese and stir until it melts. Turn off the heat. Add remaining salt and pepper or to taste.
5. Transfer the roasted Brussels sprouts into a smaller baking dish. Pour sauce on top. Scatter bacon bits and remaining cheese.
6. Bake until the sauce is bubbling.

3. Taco Breakfast Skillet

Cooking time: 30 minutes

Number of servings: 3

Nutritional values per serving:

- Calories – 563
- Fat – 44 g
- Total Carbohydrate – 9 g
- Digestible carbohydrate – 5 g
- Edible fibers – 4 g
- Protein – 32 g

Ingredients:

- ½ pound ground beef
- 1/3 cup water
- ¾ cup shredded sharp cheddar cheese, divided
- 1 small Roma tomato, diced
- 1/8 cup sliced black olives
- 2 tablespoons sour cream
- 1 small avocado, peeled, pitted, cut into cubes
- ½ jalapeño, sliced (optional)
- 2 tablespoons taco seasoning
- 5 large eggs

- 2 tablespoons heavy cream
- 1 green onion, sliced
- 2 tablespoons salsa
- 2 tablespoons chopped cilantro

Directions:

1. Add beef into an ovenproof skillet and place the skillet over medium-high flame. Cook until brown. Discard extra fat from the pan.
2. Add water and taco seasoning into the pan. Mix well. Lower the heat and cook until thick. Stir occasionally. Turn off the heat.
3. Transfer half the beef mixture into a bowl.
4. Whisk eggs and heavy cream in a bowl. Add ½ cup cheese and whisk well. Transfer this mixture into the skillet. Mix well.
5. Place the skillet in a preheated oven.
6. Bake at 375° F for about 30 minutes or until cooked.
7. Spread remaining beef (that was set aside) over the baked meat. Sprinkle ¼ cup cheese on top.
8. Scatter avocado, tomatoes, and olives. Spoon salsa and sour cream on top.
9. Sprinkle cilantro, green onions, and jalapeño on top and serve.

4. Keto Oatmeal

Cooking time: 5 minutes

Number of servings: 2

Nutritional values per serving: Without toppings

- Calories – 453
- Fat – 36 g
- Total Carbohydrate – 15 g
- Digestible carbohydrate – 5 g
- Edible fibers – 10 g
- Protein – 18 g

Ingredients:

- 4 tablespoons hemp hearts
- 4 tablespoons unsweetened shredded coconut
- 4 tablespoons almond flour
- 2 tablespoons golden flaxseed meal
- ½ teaspoon granulated stevia / erythritol blend
- 1 teaspoon pure vanilla extract
- 2 tablespoons chia seeds
- 1/8 teaspoon salt
- 1 cup water

Directions:

1. Combine all the ingredients except vanilla extract in a saucepan.
2. Place the saucepan over low flame. Stir constantly until thick.
3. Add vanilla and stir.
4. Divide into 3 bowls and serve with any keto-friendly toppings of your choice, if desired.

5. Keto Dutch Baby

Cooking time: 10 minutes

Number of servings: 2

Nutritional values per serving: ½ pancake

- Calories – 334
- Fat – 30 g
- Total Carbohydrate – 8 g
- Digestible carbohydrate – 4 g
- Edible fibers – 4 g
- Protein – 12 g

Ingredients:

For pancake:

- 6 tablespoons almond flour
- 1/8 teaspoon salt
- 6 tablespoons unsweetened almond milk
- 2 teaspoons butter
- 2 eggs
- ½ teaspoon pure vanilla extract
- 2 teaspoons swerve granulated

For topping:

- 1-ounce macadamia nuts, chopped
- 12 blackberries

Directions:

1. Place an ovenproof skillet over low flame. Let it heat. Turn off the heat.
2. Add the remaining ingredients for pancake into a blender and blend it until it becomes smooth.
3. Add butter. When butter melts, turn off the heat and swirl the pan so that butter spreads. Pour batter into the skillet.
4. Bake at 400° F for about 10 minutes or until cooked.
5. Cut into 2 halves and place one half on each plate. Scatter macadamia and blackberries on top and serve.

6. Mini Pancake Donuts

Cooking time: 5 minutes per batch

Number of servings: 44 mini donuts

Nutritional values per serving: 1 mini donut

- Calories – 32
- Fat – 2.7 g
- Total Carbohydrate – 0.8 g
- Digestible carbohydrate – 0.53 g
- Edible fibers – 0.27 g
- Protein – 1.4 g

Ingredients:

- 6 ounces cream cheese
- ½ cup almond flour
- 2 teaspoons baking powder
- 2 tablespoons coconut flour
- 2 teaspoons vanilla extract
- 20 drops stevia
- 6 large eggs
- 8 tablespoons erythritol
- Coconut oil spray

Directions:

1. Add cream cheese, almond flour, baking powder, coconut flour, vanilla, stevia, eggs, and erythritol into a mixing bowl. Beat with a stick blender until it becomes smooth.
2. Preheat a mini donut maker, following the instructions of the manufacturer. Spray the donut maker with coconut oil spray. Spoon batter into the wells of the donut maker.
3. Cook for 3 minutes. Turn over the donuts. Cook for 2 minutes
4. Remove donuts from the donut maker.
5. Repeat steps 2-4 and cook the remaining donuts.

7. Mushroom Omelet

Cooking time: 3 - 5 minutes

Number of servings: 2

Nutritional values per serving: ½ an omelet

- Calories – 517
- Fat – 44 g
- Total Carbohydrate – 5 g
- Digestible carbohydrate – 4 g
- Edible fibers – 1 g
- Protein – 26 g

Ingredients:

- 6 eggs
- 2 ounces shredded cheese
- 8 large mushrooms, sliced
- 2 ounces butter, to fry
- ½ yellow onion, chopped
- Salt, as per taste
- Pepper, as per taste

Directions:

1. Beat eggs with salt and pepper.
2. Place a nonstick pan over medium flame. Add butter. When butter melts, add onions and mushrooms and cook until tender.
3. Spread the vegetables in the pan. Pour the beaten eggs over the vegetables. Do not stir.
4. When the eggs are nearly cooked, scatter cheese all over the omelet.
5. Fold over the omelet in half. When the underside is golden brown, remove the omelet from the pan.
6. Cut into 2 halves and serve.

8. Breakfast Bowl

Cooking time: 30 minutes

Number of servings: 2

Nutritional values per serving:

- Calories – 617
- Fat – 49 g
- Total Carbohydrate – 7 g
- Digestible carbohydrate – 4 g
- Edible fibers – 3 g
- Protein – 32 g

Ingredients:

- 2 large eggs
- 14 ounces radishes, cut into bite-size pieces
- ½ cup shredded cheddar cheese
- ½ teaspoon pink Himalayan salt
- ½ teaspoon pepper
- 7 ounces ground sausage

Directions:

1. Place a skillet over medium-high flame and add the sausage. Cook it thoroughly.
2. Remove the sausage and set it aside on a plate. Let the fat released while cooking remain in the pan.
3. Add radish, salt, and pepper and sauté until fork tender. Turn off the heat. Divide into 2 bowls.
4. Meanwhile, cook the eggs to the desired doneness.
5. Spread half the sausage over the radishes in each bowl. Sprinkle half the cheese over the sausage in each bowl. In a few minutes, the cheese will melt with the heat of the sausages.
6. Place a cooked egg on top of each bowl and serve.

9. Keto Breakfast "Potatoes"

Cooking time: 12 – 15 minutes

Number of servings: 8

Nutritional values per serving:

- Calories – 123
- Fat – 10 g
- Total Carbohydrate – 6 g
- Digestible carbohydrate – 5 g
- Edible fibers – 1 g
- Protein – 3 g

Ingredients:

- 2 large turnips, peeled, diced
- 6 slices bacon, chopped
- 1 teaspoon garlic powder
- 1 teaspoon paprika
- Salt to taste
- Pepper to taste
- Fresh parsley, chopped, to garnish
- 1 medium onion, diced
- 2 tablespoons ghee or avocado oil
- 2 green onions, sliced, to garnish

Directions:

1. Place a large skillet over medium-high flame. Add the oil in it and then the turnip and all the spices and sauté for about 5 minutes.
2. Stir the onions and sauté until translucent.
3. Add the bacon and cook until the bacon turns crisp. Stir occasionally.
4. Garnish with green onions and parsley and serve.

10. Tomatoes and Cheese Frittata

Cooking time: 12 – 15 minutes

Number of servings: 4

Nutritional values per serving: ¼ frittata

- Calories – 435
- Fat – 32.6 g
- Total Carbohydrate – 7.4 g
- Digestible carbohydrate – 6.2 g
- Edible fibers – 1.2 g
- Protein – 26.7 g

Ingredients:

- 12 large eggs
- 1 1/3 cups crumbled soft cheese like feta cheese
- 2 tablespoons ghee
- Freshly ground pepper
- Salt to taste
- 1 medium white onion, sliced
- 1 1/3 cups halved cherry tomatoes
- ¼ cup chopped, fresh herbs of your choice

Directions:

1. Preheat the oven to 400° F.
2. Beat eggs with salt and pepper. Whisk in the herbs.
3. Place an ovenproof skillet over medium flame and pour the ghee. When the ghee melts, add onion and sauté until brown.
4. Add beaten eggs and cook until the edges are slightly set.
5. Scatter cheese and tomatoes over the eggs. Turn off the heat.
6. Transfer the skillet into the oven. Broil until the eggs are set.
7. Take out the skillet from the oven and cool for a few minutes. Cut into quarters and serve.

11. Bacon and Zucchini Hash

Cooking time: 25 minutes

Number of servings: 2

Nutritional values per serving:

- Calories – 423
- Fat – 35.5 g
- Total Carbohydrate – 9.1 g
- Digestible carbohydrate – 6.6 g
- Edible fibers – 2.5 g
- Protein – 17.4 g

Ingredients:

- 2 medium zucchinis, chopped into medium size pieces
- 1 small white onion, finely chopped
- 2 tablespoons chopped parsley
- 2 large eggs, cooked sunny side up
- Salt and pepper to taste
- 2 tablespoons ghee or coconut oil
- 4 slices bacon

Directions:

1. Place a skillet over medium flame. Add the bacon and cook it until light brown.
2. Add zucchini and cook until tender
3. Add parsley, stir and remove from heat.
4. Divide into 2 plates. Top each with an egg and serve.

12. Cinnamon Swirl Bread

Cooking time: 50 – 60 minutes

Number of servings: 24

Nutritional values per serving: 1 slice

- Calories – 174
- Fat – 17 g
- Total Carbohydrate – 5 g
- Digestible carbohydrate – 3 g
- Edible fibers – 2 g
- Protein – 5 g

Ingredients:

For cinnamon mix:

- 2 teaspoons ground cinnamon
- 2 tablespoons Pyure all-purpose

Wet ingredients:

- 1 cup butter, melted
- 14 large eggs
- 6 tablespoons melted coconut oil
- 2 teaspoons vanilla extract

Dry ingredients:

- 1 1/3 cups almond flour
- 1 teaspoon xanthan gum
- ½ teaspoon stevia extract powder
- 2 teaspoons baking powder
- 2/3 cup coconut flour
- 1 teaspoon salt
- 2 teaspoons ground cinnamon
- 1 cup swerve or erythritol

Directions:

1. To make cinnamon mix: Add pyure and cinnamon in a bowl. Stir and set aside.
2. For bread batter: Add all the dry ingredients into a bowl and stir until well combined.
3. Place the wet ingredients into the food processor bowl and pulse it thoroughly until well incorporated.
4. Add the dry ingredients into a bowl and stir until well combined. Transfer the mixture of dry ingredients into the food processor bowl and mix until well incorporated and free from lumps.

5. Take out 1 cup of the batter and add into the cinnamon mix. Stir and set aside.
6. Take 2 loaf pans (9 x 5 inches each) and line with parchment paper. Divide half the bread batter into each of the pans. Spread it evenly.
7. Divide half the cinnamon mix batter among the loaf pans and spread over the bread batter.
8. Divide the remaining bread batter and spread over the cinnamon batter layer. Divide the remaining cinnamon mix batter and spread over the bread batter layer. Take a knife and swirl the batter lightly.
9. Place the baking dish in a in a preheated oven and bake at 350° F for 40 minutes.
10. Lower the temperature to 325° F. If the top of the bread is getting brown and is not cooked inside, then cover the loaf pan with foil. Bake for 15 minutes or until a blunt knife when inserted in the middle of the bread comes out clean.
11. Let the loaf pans remain in the oven for 10-15 minutes before taking it out of the oven.
12. Cut each loaf into 12 equal slices and serve.

13. Blueberry Pancakes

Cooking time: 132 minutes

Number of servings: 6

Nutritional values per serving:

- Calories – 132
- Fat – 7 g
- Total Carbohydrate – 4.1 g
- Digestible carbohydrate – 3 g
- Edible fibers – 2 g
- Protein – 0 g

Ingredients:

- ¼ cup coconut flour
- 1 cup almond flour
- 2 teaspoons baking powder
- 2 teaspoons ground cinnamon
- 3-4 tablespoons granulated swerve or erythritol
- ½ cup almond milk or any other milk of your choice
- 6 large eggs
- ½ cup blueberries, preferably frozen and thawed

Directions:

1. Add all ingredients except blueberries into a blender. Blend well until a thick batter is formed.
2. Transfer into a mixing bowl. Add blueberries and stir well. Cover and let it rest for 10 minutes.
3. Put a nonstick pan over medium-low heat. Spray some cooking spray. When the pan is heated, pour 1/6 of the batter (about ¼ cup) on the pan. Swirl the pan slightly to spread the batter. Cover the pan.
4. Let it cook until the bottom of the pancake is golden brown. Flip sides and cook until golden brown.
5. Remove pancake and keep warm in an oven.
6. Repeat steps 3-5 and make the remaining pancakes and serve.

14. Triple Berry Avocado Breakfast Smoothie

Cooking time: 10 minutes

Number of servings: 2

Nutritional values per serving:

- Calories – 330
- Fat – 26 g
- Total Carbohydrate – 21 g
- Digestible carbohydrate – 9 g
- Edible fibers – 12 g
- Protein – 12 g

Ingredients:

- 1 cup frozen mixed berries (strawberries, raspberries, and blueberries)
- 4 cups chopped spinach
- 1 medium avocado, peeled, pitted, chopped
- 2 cups water
- 4 tablespoons hemp seeds

Directions:

1. Add berries, spinach, avocado, water, and hemp seeds in a blender. Blend for about a minute or until it's all well combined.
2. Pour the smoothie in tall glasses. Serve cold or put some crushed ice if desired.

15. Chocolate Peanut Butter Smoothie

Cooking time: 10 minutes

Number of servings: 2

Nutritional values per serving:

- Calories – 345
- Fat – 31 g
- Total Carbohydrate – 13 g
- Digestible carbohydrate – 9 g
- Edible fibers – 4 g
- Protein – 11 g

Ingredients:

- 2 cups unsweetened almond milk
- 2 tablespoons cocoa powder, unsweetened
- 2 cups ice cubes
- 4 tablespoons creamy peanut butter
- ½ cup heavy cream

Directions:

1. Add milk, cocoa, ice, peanut butter, and cream into a blender. Blend for about a minute or until it's all well combined.
2. Pour the smoothie in glasses and serve cold.

Chapter Seven: Ketogenic Lunch Recipes

1. Grilled Chicken Salad

Cooking time: 6 – 8 minutes

Number of servings: 4

Nutritional values per serving:

- Calories – 617
- Fat – 52 g
- Total Carbohydrate – 11 g
- Digestible carbohydrate – 7 g
- Edible fibers – 4 g
- Protein – 30 g

Ingredients:

- 1 pound chicken thighs, grilled, sliced
- ½ cup chopped cherry tomatoes
- 1 medium avocado, peeled, pitted, sliced
- 8 cups chopped romaine lettuce

- 1 medium cucumber, thinly sliced
- 2 ounces feta cheese, crumbled
- 4 tablespoons red wine vinegar
- 2 ounces olives, pitted, sliced
- 6 tablespoons extra-virgin olive oil
- Salt to taste
- Pepper to taste
- 2 teaspoons chopped fresh thyme
- 2 teaspoons minced garlic

Directions:

1. Sprinkle salt, pepper, thyme, and garlic over the chicken.
2. Place a skillet with oil over medium-high flame. As the oil heats, add the chicken and cook it until it gets brown. Remove from the flame and set aside.
3. Add tomatoes, lettuce, olives, avocado, and cucumber into a bowl and toss well.
4. Place chicken on top. Pour vinegar on top and serve.

2. Curried Cabbage Coconut Salad

Cooking time: 20 minutes

Number of servings: 8

Nutritional values per serving:

- Calories – 309
- Fat – 29 g
- Total Carbohydrate – 12 g
- Digestible carbohydrate – 6 g
- Edible fibers – 6 g
- Protein – 12 g

Ingredients:

- 1 head cabbage, medium finely shredded
- Juice of 2 lemons
- ½ cup tamari sauce
- 1 teaspoon ground ginger
- 1 teaspoon curry powder
- 2/3 cup dried or desiccated coconut, unsweetened
- ½ cup coconut oil
- 6 teaspoons sesame powder
- 1 teaspoon ground cumin

Directions:

1. Add cabbage, lemon juice, tamari, ginger, curry powder, coconut, coconut oil, sesame powder, and cumin into a large bowl. Toss well.
2. Refrigerate for an hour.
3. Toss again before serving.

3. Keto "Potato" Salad

Cooking time: 20 minutes

Number of servings: 4

Nutritional values per serving:

- Calories – 254
- Fat – 21.1 g
- Total Carbohydrate – 10.5 g
- Digestible carbohydrate – 7.6 g
- Edible fibers – 2.9 g
- Protein – 6.6 g

Ingredients:

For dressing:

- ½ teaspoon Dijon mustard
- Freshly ground pepper to taste
- 6 tablespoons unsweetened mayonnaise
- 1 tablespoon pickle juice or vinegar
- Salt to taste
- ½ teaspoon celery seeds
- 1 tablespoon chopped chives
- 2 tablespoons chopped fresh parsley

For salad:

- 8.5 ounces rutabaga, chopped into ½ inch pieces
- 2.7 ounces celeriac, peeled, cut into ½ inch pieces
- 3 large eggs
- 8.8 ounces turnip peeled, cut into ½ inch pieces
- ½ small onion (about 1.25 ounces), finely chopped
- 2.1 ounces pickled cucumber, diced
- 1 ounce celery stalk, sliced
- ½ tablespoon apple cider vinegar
- 1 bay leaf
- ½ teaspoons black peppercorns

Directions:

1. To cook eggs: Add eggs into a saucepan. Fill the saucepan with water and place the saucepan over medium flame. Bring to a boil. Let it boil for 10 minutes. Turn off the heat and drain off the water. Immerse the eggs in a bowl of cold water.

2. Peel and cut each of the eggs into 4 pieces.

3. For salad: Place a pot of water with vinegar, peppercorns, salt, and bay leaves over medium flame.

4. When it begins to boil, add rutabaga, turnips, and celeriac.

5. When it comes to a boil again, lower the heat and simmer until vegetables are tender. Collect the spices and throw it off. Drain off the water.

6. Transfer the cooked vegetables into a bowl and set aside to cool.

7. Add onion, pickled cucumber, celery, and eggs into the bowl of cooked vegetables and toss well.

8. Add all ingredients for dressing into the bowl of salad and stir until well combined.

9. Serve.

4. Turmeric & Cauliflower Soup

Cooking time: 25 – 35 minutes

Number of servings: 3

Nutritional values per serving:

- Calories – 471
- Fat – 34 g
- Total Carbohydrate – 9.5 g
- Digestible carbohydrate – 5.6 g
- Edible fibers – 3.9 g
- Protein – 32.5 g

Ingredients:

- 1 medium head cauliflower, cut into chunks
- 1 inch ginger, halved
- Pepper to taste
- Salt to taste
- 1 medium carrot, cut into chunks
- 1 tablespoon turmeric powder
- ½ cup coconut milk
- 4 cups water

For crispy tofu croutons:

- ½ pound extra-firm tofu, cut into 16 equal pieces
- ¼ teaspoon ground cumin
- ½ tablespoon soy sauce
- ½ teaspoon smoked paprika
- ½ tablespoon olive oil
- ½ teaspoon lemon juice

To serve:

- ½ cup full fat coconut milk
- Freshly ground pepper to taste
- Dried herbs of your choice, to garnish

Directions:

1. Pour water into a soup pot and place the pot over medium-high flame. When water begins to boil, add ginger, carrot and cauliflower. Cook until the vegetables are soft. Remove from heat and let it cool.
2. Meanwhile, make the crispy tofu as follows: Add all ingredients for crispy tofu into a bowl and toss well. Spread the tofu evenly on a lined baking sheet.

3. Place the baking sheet in a preheated oven and bake at 400° F for 20 minutes or until crisp.
4. When the soup is cooled, transfer into a blender and blend well. Pour the soup back into the pot. Add seasonings, turmeric, and coconut milk and whisk well. Heat thoroughly. Remove from heat and allow it to rest for 10 minutes.
5. Ladle into soup bowls. Top with crispy tofu and coconut milk. Sprinkle pepper and dried herbs on top and serve.

5. Roasted Tomato Soup

Cooking time: 40 minutes

Number of servings: 3

Nutritional values per serving:

- Calories −95
- Fat − 6 g
- Total Carbohydrate − 9 g
- Digestible carbohydrate − 6 g
- Edible fibers − 3 g
- Protein − 2 g

Ingredients:

- 5 medium Roma tomatoes, chopped into 1-inch cubes
- 2 cloves garlic, minced
- 2 tablespoons heavy cream
- Sea salt to taste
- Pepper to taste
- ½ tablespoon olive oil
- 2-3 tablespoons water
- Fresh basil, minced

Directions:

1. Place a sheet of aluminum foil on a baking sheet. Grease it lightly with cooking spray.
2. Add tomatoes, garlic, and oil into a bowl and toss well. Transfer onto the prepared baking sheet. Spread it without overlapping.
3. Place the baking sheet in a preheated oven and roast at 400° F for 20-25 or until the skin is lightly charred at a few places.
4. Take out the baking sheet from the oven and cool for a while. Add the tomatoes and garlic into a blender along with the cooked juices. Blend it well until it becomes smooth. Pour it into a soup pot. Place the pot over medium flame. Add salt, pepper, and water and stir. Heat thoroughly.
5. Add cream and basil. Stir and turn off heat.
6. Ladle into soup bowls and serve.

6. One Pot Creamy Meatball Soup

Cooking time: 45 minutes

Number of servings: 7

Nutritional values per serving:

- Calories – 756
- Fat – 59 g
- Total Carbohydrate – 19 g
- Digestible carbohydrate – 15 g
- Edible fibers – 4 g
- Protein – 38 g

Ingredients:

For meatballs:

- ½ pound ground Italian sausage
- ½ pound ground pork
- ¼ cup finely minced onions
- ½ stalk celery, finely minced
- ½ tablespoon minced garlic
- 1 small egg

For soup:

- 1 medium onion, diced
- 4 ounces cremini mushrooms, cut into thin rounds
- 1 large carrot, peeled, cut into thin rounds
- 2 tablespoons diced garlic
- Salt to taste
- Pepper to taste
- 3 small stalks celery, cut into thin half moons
- ½ tablespoon Italian herb seasoning blend
- ½ cup grated parmesan cheese
- 6 ounces beef stock
- 1 cup heavy whipping cream

Directions:

1. To make meatballs: Add all ingredients for meatballs into a bowl and mix well.
2. Make small balls (about 2 inches in diameter) of the mixture. Place on a baking sheet. Refrigerate for an hour.
3. To make soup: Place a soup pot over medium flame. Add the oil, and once it's heated, add the meatballs and cook until they brown. Remove meatballs and place them on paper plates.

4. Add vegetables into the pot and simmer until vegetables are slightly cooked.
5. Stir in the herbs, stock, and meatballs. Raise the heat to high flame. Cook until the liquid in the pot is reduced to half its original quantity. Remove from heat.
6. Lower the heat and add cream, whisking simultaneously while adding.
7. Place the pot over medium flame. Add parmesan cheese and whisk well. Cook until thick.
8. Ladle into soup bowls and serve.

7. Skillet Pizza

Cooking time: 30 minutes

Number of servings: 2

Nutritional values per serving: ½ a pizza

- Calories – 606
- Fat – 50 g
- Total Carbohydrate – 6 g
- Digestible carbohydrate – 5 g
- Edible fibers – 1 g
- Protein – 33 g

Ingredients:

- 6 ounces mozzarella cheese, shredded
- 2 ounces pepperoni slices
- 1 teaspoon Italian seasoning
- 4 ounces fresh sausage, cooked, crumbled
- 2 ounces green bell pepper, chopped
- 4 tablespoons unsweetened tomato sauce

Directions:

1. Place a nonstick over medium flame. Retain ¼ of the cheese and scatter the rest of the cheese on the bottom of the skillet. In a few minutes, the cheese will melt.
2. Reduce the heat to low heat. Scatter sausage, bell pepper, and retained cheese over the cheese crust.
3. Place pepperoni slices on top. Continue cooking for a few minutes until the crust is brown.
4. Garnish with Italian seasoning. Remove from heat. Let it rest for 5 minutes.
5. Cut into 2 halves and serve.

8. Zucchini Boats

Cooking time: 30 – 40 minutes

Number of servings: 4

Nutritional values per serving:

- Calories – 693
- Fat – 62 g
- Total Carbohydrate – 5 g
- Digestible carbohydrate – 3 g
- Edible fibers – 2 g
- Protein – 27 g

Ingredients:

- 2 medium zucchinis
- Salt to taste
- Freshly ground pepper to taste
- 16 ounces goat cheese
- 4 cloves garlic, peeled, thinly sliced
- 8 tablespoons olive oil
- 3 ounces baby spinach
- 4 tablespoons marinara sauce

Directions:

1. Scoop the seeds from the zucchini using a spoon. Your zucchini boats are now ready. Do not discard the seeds. Roughly chop the seeds. Place zucchini boats on a baking sheet.
2. Place a skillet with ¼ cup oil over medium flame. When the oil heats, add garlic and stir constantly until it turns light brown.
3. Throw in the spinach and chopped zucchini seeds and cook until the zucchini seeds are tender. Add salt and pepper to taste.
4. Spread a tablespoon of marinara sauce inside each of the zucchini boats. Divide the spinach and zucchini seeds mixture and fill the boats with it.
5. Scatter goat cheese on top.
6. Place in a preheated oven and bake at 375° F for around 25 minutes or until zucchini is tender.
7. Dribble remaining oil on top. Sprinkle pepper on and serve.

9. Chicken Stir-Fry with Shirataki Noodles

Cooking time: 15 minutes

Number of servings: 4

Nutritional values per serving:

- Calories –737
- Fat – 63 g
- Total Carbohydrate – 12 g
- Digestible carbohydrate – 8 g
- Edible fibers – 4 g
- Protein – 32 g

Ingredients:

- 1 pound shirataki noodles
- 6 tablespoons coconut oil or light olive oil
- 10 ounces oyster mushrooms
- Salt to taste
- Freshly ground pepper to taste
- 1 ½ pounds boneless chicken thighs or breasts, sliced into strips
- 6 ounces celery stalks, sliced

- 1 orange or yellow bell peppers, sliced

For hot sauce:

- 4 tablespoons sesame oil or light olive oil
- 2 tablespoons rice vinegar or cider vinegar
- 2 tablespoons sriracha sauce
- ¼ cup water
- 2 tablespoons tamari
- 2 cloves garlic, peeled, minced

Directions:

1. Rinse the noodles in a colander with running water. Make sure you rinse it well. You need to get rid of the water in which the noodles come. Rinse for at least 2 minutes.
2. Place a wok over medium flame. Add the oil, and once it's heated, add chicken and sauté for a few minutes until chicken is cooked. Add salt and pepper as needed.
3. Stir in the noodles and vegetables. Heat thoroughly.
4. To make hot sauce: Whisk together all the ingredients for sauce in a bowl.
5. Pour half the sauce into the wok and toss well.
6. Divide onto 4 plates. Drizzle remaining sauce on top and serve.

10. Salmon Pie

Cooking time: 40 minutes

Number of servings: 80

Nutritional values per serving:

- Calories – 1,056
- Fat – 97 g
- Total Carbohydrate – 13 g
- Digestible carbohydrate – 6 g
- Edible fibers – 7 g
- Protein – 34 g

Ingredients:

For pie crust:

- 1 ½ cups almond flour
- 8 tablespoons coconut flour
- 2 teaspoons baking powder
- 6 tablespoons olive oil or coconut water
- ¼ cup water
- 8 tablespoons sesame seeds
- 2 tablespoons ground psyllium husk powder
- 1/8 teaspoon salt

- 2 eggs

For filling:

- 16 ounces smoked salmon
- 6 eggs
- 1 teaspoon onion powder
- 10 ounces cream cheese
- 2 cups keto-friendly mayonnaise
- ¼ cup finely chopped fresh dill
- Pepper to taste
- 10 ounces shredded cheese
- Salt to taste (optional)

Directions:

1. To make pie crust: Combine all the ingredients for the crust and add it into the food processor bowl. Process until well combined and a ball of dough is formed.
2. Line a 10-inch springform pan with parchment paper.
3. Place the dough in the pan and press the dough (with greased hands) into the pan, on the bottom as well as the sides.

4. Place the pan in a preheated oven and bake at 350° F for around 12 to 15 minutes or until light brown.
5. To make filling: Combine all the ingredients except salmon in a bowl. Spread this mixture over the pie crust. Place salmon on top.
6. Place the pan back in the oven and bake until golden brown.
7. Remove from the oven and cool for 5 minutes. Cut into wedges and serve.

11. Salmon-Filled Avocados

Cooking time: 10 minutes

Number of servings: 4

Nutritional values per serving:

- Calories – 717
- Fat – 65 g
- Total Carbohydrate – 19 g
- Digestible carbohydrate – 6 g
- Edible fibers – 13 g
- Protein – 22 g

Ingredients:

- 4 avocados, halved, pitted
- 1 ½ cups crème fraiche or sour cream
- 4 tablespoons lemon juice (optional)
- 12 ounces smoked salmon
- Salt to taste
- Pepper to taste

Directions:

1. Fill the cavities of the avocado halves with crème fraiche.
2. Place smoked salmon on top. Sprinkle salt and pepper to taste.
3. Drizzle lemon juice on top. This is done to prevent the avocado from being brown.
4. Serve.

12. Bacon Avocado Sandwich

Cooking time: 15 minutes

Number of servings: 12

Nutritional values per serving: ½ a sandwich

- Calories – 405.55
- Fat – 31.02 g
- Total Carbohydrate – 6.72 g
- Digestible carbohydrate – 4.31 g
- Edible fibers – 2.42 g
- Protein – 24.8 g

Ingredients:

For keto cloud bread:

- 6 large eggs
- ¼ teaspoon cream of tartar
- 1 teaspoon garlic powder
- 6 ounces cream cheese, cubed
- ½ teaspoon salt

For filling:

- 6 tablespoons keto-friendly mayonnaise
- 12 slices bacon
- 12 slices pepper Jack cheese
- 12 ounces avocado, mashed
- 6 teaspoons sriracha
- 18 ounces chicken breast
- 12 whole grape tomatoes
- Salt to taste
- Pepper to taste

Directions:

1. Separate the whites and the yolks into 2 bowls. Add salt and cream of tartar to the bowl of whites. Beat with an electric hand mixer until frothy and slightly soft peaks are visible.
2. Add cream cheese to the bowl of yolks and beat until light yellow in color.
3. Add half the whites into the bowl of yolks and fold gently. Add remaining whites and fold again.
4. Line a large baking sheet with parchment paper. Pour ¼ cup batter on one side of the baking sheet. Shape into a square. This is one bread slice. Similarly, make 11 more bread slices on the baking sheet. Use 2 baking sheets if required.

5. Sprinkle garlic powder on top of the bread slices.
6. Bake in a preheated oven at 300° F for around 25 minutes.
7. Meanwhile, season the chicken and bacon with salt and pepper.
8. Place a skillet with bacon over medium flame. Add salt and pepper and cook to your preference.
9. Remove bacon and set aside.
10. Add chicken into the skillet and cook until done. Turn off the heat and let it cool for a few minutes.
11. Cut chicken into slices.
12. To assemble: Add mayonnaise and sriracha sauce into a bowl and stir. Spread mayonnaise mixture on the bottom side of 6 cloud breads.
13. Layer each with 2 slices cheese and 2 slices bacon (place on the mayonnaise side). Place 2 grape tomato halves on each. Divide the mashed avocado and spread on top.
14. Cover with remaining cloud bread. Cut each into 2 halves and serve.

13. Coconut Lime Noodles with Chili Tamari Tofu

Cooking time: 15 minutes

Number of servings: 2

Nutritional values per serving:

- Calories – 374.3
- Fat – 31.1 g
- Total Carbohydrate – 9.1 g
- Digestible carbohydrate – 3.6 g
- Edible fibers – 3.6 g
- Protein – 15.7 g

Ingredients:

For noodles:

- ½ can (from a 13.5-ounce can) full fat coconut milk
- 2 tablespoons sesame seeds
- ¼ teaspoon ground ginger or use ½ teaspoon grated ginger
- Salt to taste
- 1 package (8 ounces) shirataki noodles

- Juice of ½ lime
- Zest of ½ lime, grated + extra to garnish
- A large pinch red pepper flakes, to garnish

For tofu:

- 7 ounces extra firm tofu, drained, pressed of excess moisture, cut into 1" cubes
- ½ tablespoon olive oil
- 2 tablespoons low sodium tamari
- Cayenne pepper to taste

Directions:

1. Place tofu in a shallow dish in a single layer. Add oil, tamari, and cayenne pepper in a bowl and whisk well. Pour over the tofu. Turn the pieces a few times so that it is well-coated.
2. Spread the tofu pieces on a baking sheet, without overlapping.
3. Place the baking sheet in a preheated oven and bake at 350° F for about 20-25 minutes.
4. Meanwhile, drain the noodles. Rinse the noodles well and add into a wok or skillet.
5. Place the skillet over medium flame. Add the remaining ingredients for the noodles and mix well. Cover the pan partially and cook for 6-7 minutes.

6. Lower the heat and cook for 6-8 minutes. Turn off the heat. Cool for a while.
7. Serve noodles on individual serving plates. Place tofu on top. Sprinkle lime zest and red pepper flakes and serve.

14. Quesadillas

Cooking time: 15 minutes

Number of servings:

Nutritional values per serving:

- Calories – 431
- Fat – 33 g
- Total Carbohydrate – 7 g
- Digestible carbohydrate – 4 g
- Edible fibers – 3 g
- Protein – 27 g

Ingredients:

For quesadillas:

- 2 ½ cups shredded mozzarella cheese
- 4 tablespoons coconut flour
- 2 eggs
- 2 tablespoons heavy cream
- ½ teaspoon Italian seasoning (optional)

For the filling:

- 4 tablespoons chopped jalapeño peppers

- 1 cup shredded cheddar cheese

Directions:

1. To make tortillas: Add cheese into a microwave safe dish. Microwave for a few seconds until the cheese melts. Do not heat for too long.
2. Add the remaining ingredients to the melted cheese and mix well into dough. You can knead for a few minutes.
3. Divide the dough into 4 equal portions and shape each portion into a ball. If the balls are too hard, then microwave for 10-15 seconds, to soften.
4. Place a ball in between 2 sheets of parchment paper and roll into a circle.
5. Carefully place on a baking sheet.
6. Repeat with the remaining balls.
7. Place the baking sheet in a preheated oven and bake at 350° F for about 10 minutes.
8. When the tortilla cools, divide and sprinkle cheese and jalapeño over it.
9. Bake for a few more minutes until the cheese melts.
10. Serve hot.

15. Keto Burgers

Cooking time: 15 minutes

Number of servings: 6

Nutritional values per serving:

- Calories – 531
- Fat – 45 g
- Total Carbohydrate – 5 g
- Digestible carbohydrate – 4 g
- Edible fibers – 1 g
- Protein – 26 g

Ingredients:

- 2 pounds ground beef
- 2 tablespoons McCormick's Montreal steak seasoning
- 2 tablespoons Worcestershire sauce
- Salt to taste
- Pepper to taste
- 8 ounces onion, sliced
- 4 tablespoons olive oil + extra to grease the grates
- 1 teaspoon erythritol

Directions:

1. Place beef in a bowl and break the meat. Add Worcestershire sauce and steak seasoning and mix well.
2. Add 2 tablespoons of oil and mix well.
3. Divide the meat into 6 equal portions and shape each into a patty. Make a dent in the center of each patty.
4. Take out your grill and clean the grates before preheating. Grease the grill grates. Sprinkle salt and pepper over the burgers. Place on the grill and cook to your preference.
5. Meanwhile, make the caramelized onions as follows: Place a skillet over medium-low heat. Add remaining oil (after greasing the grill grates), onion, and erythritol and cook until onions turn golden brown. Stir occasionally.,
6. Divide the caramelized onions and spoon over burgers.
7. Serve.

Chapter Eight: Ketogenic Snack Recipes

1. Cheddar Cheese and Bacon Balls

Cooking time: 8-10 minutes

Number of servings: 16

Nutritional values per serving: 3 balls

- Calories – 274
- Fat – 26 g
- Total Carbohydrate – 2 g
- Digestible carbohydrate – 2 g
- Edible fibers – 0 g
- Protein – 8 g

Ingredients:

- 1 teaspoon chili flakes (optional)
- 10 ounces bacon
- 10 ounces cheddar cheese
- 10 ounces cream cheese

- 2 tablespoons butter
- 4 ounces butter, at room temperature
- 1 teaspoon pepper (optional)

Directions:

1. Place a pan over medium flame. Add the butter and allow it to melt. Add bacon and cook until crisp Remove the bacon, and when it is cool enough to handle, crumble it. Set aside in a shallow bowl.
2. Pour the remaining fat from the pan into a bowl. Add cheddar cheese, cream cheese, 4 ounces butter, chili flakes, and pepper and mix well, using your hands.
3. Chill for 20-30 minutes.
4. Divide the mixture into 48 equal portions and shape into balls.
5. Dredge the mixture in bacon and serve.

2. Smoked Salmon Appetizer

Cooking time: 15 minutes

Number of servings: 12

Nutritional values per serving:

- Calories – 255
- Fat – 23 g
- Total Carbohydrate – 3 g
- Digestible carbohydrate – 3 g
- Edible fibers – 0 g
- Protein – 9 g

Ingredients:

- 14 ounces smoked salmon, cut into small pieces
- 2/3 cup keto-friendly mayonnaise
- Zest of a lemon, grated
- 16 ounces cream cheese
- ½ cup chopped fresh dill or fresh chives
- ½ teaspoon pepper
- 12 lettuce leaves, to serve

Directions:

1. Add salmon, mayonnaise, lemon zest, cream cheese, dill, and pepper into a bowl and toss well. Cover the bowl and chill for 15 minutes.
2. Place the lettuce leaves on a large serving platter. Toss well. Divide the salmon mixture among the lettuce leaves and place on top of the lettuce leaves.
3. Serve.

3. Chocolate Cranberry Muffins

Cooking time: 15 minutes

Number of servings: 12

Nutritional values per serving:

- Calories – 221
- Fat – 19 g
- Total Carbohydrate – 8 g
- Digestible carbohydrate – 4 g
- Edible fibers – 4 g
- Protein – 6 g

Ingredients:

For dry ingredients:

- 1 cup coconut flour
- 6 tablespoons cocoa powder, unsweetened
- ½ cup Sukrin 1 or granulated Swerve
- 2 teaspoons baking powder
- ½ teaspoon salt
- ¼ teaspoon xanthan gum

<u>For wet ingredients:</u>

- ½ cup butter, softened
- 1 teaspoon vanilla extract
- ½ teaspoon stevia glycerite
- 6 large eggs
- ½ cup heavy cream
- ½ cup cream cheese, softened
- 2/3 cup cranberry relish

Directions:

1. Add all the dry ingredients into a bowl and stir until well combined.
2. Add cream cheese and butter into a mixing bowl. Beat with an electric hand mixer until creamy.
3. Beat in 2 eggs, stevia glycerite, and vanilla.
4. Add about 1/3 of the flour mixture and beat until well combined. Beat in 2 eggs.
5. Beat in half the remaining flour. Beat until creamy.
6. Beat in 2 eggs. Add the remaining flour mixture and beat until creamy.
7. Add cranberry relish and mix lightly.
8. Finally, add cream and beat until well combined.

9. Place rack in the center of the oven.

10.   Grease a 12-count muffin tin with some cooking spray. Place disposable liners in the cups.

11. Divide batter into the cups. Fill up to ¾. Pat the muffin pan lightly on the countertop to remove air bubbles, if any.

12. Bake in a preheated oven at 400° F for about 5 minutes.

13. Lower the heat to 350° F for about 20 minutes. When the muffins are ready, inserte thin skewers in the center of the muffins. They should not have any particles stuck on it to know if they are done.

14. Remove from the oven and cool for 10-15 minutes. Serve warm.

15. Unused muffins should be placed in an airtight container in the refrigerator for 3-4 days.

16. Warm the muffins in a microwave and serve.

4. Pina Colada Fat Bombs

Cooking time: 5 minutes

Number of servings: 8

Nutritional values per serving:

- Calories – 23
- Fat – 2 g
- Total Carbohydrate – 0.4 g
- Digestible carbohydrate – 0.3 g
- Edible fibers – 0.1 g
- Protein – 2 g

Ingredients:

- ½ cup coconut cream
- ½ cup water
- 2 tablespoons gelatin
- 3 teaspoons erythritol
- 1 teaspoon rum extract
- 2 teaspoons pineapple essence

Directions:

1. Pour water into a saucepan and place it over medium flame and bring to a boil. When it boils, turn off the heat.
2. Pour into a bowl. Add gelatin, erythritol, and pineapple essence and stir.
3. Let it cool for a few minutes.
4. Stir in the rum extract and coconut cream. Mix until well combined.
5. Divide into 8 fat bomb molds.
6. Set aside for some time until it sets. Remove fat bombs from the mold. Transfer into an airtight container. Refrigerate until use.

5. Jalapeño Popper Fat Bombs

Cooking time: 8-10 minutes

Number of servings: 6

Nutritional values per serving:

- Calories – 147
- Fat – 13.29 g
- Total Carbohydrate – 2.36 g
- Digestible carbohydrate – 2.13 g
- Edible fibers – 0.23 g
- Protein – 4.77 g

Ingredients:

- 6 ounces cream cheese
- 2 medium jalapeño peppers, deseeded, finely chopped
- Pepper to taste
- Salt to taste
- ½ teaspoon garlic powder
- 6 slices bacon
- 1 teaspoon dried parsley
- ½ teaspoon onion powder

Directions:

1. Add bacon into a pan. Place the pan over medium flame. Cook until crisp.
2. Place it on a plate lined with paper towels. When it becomes cool enough to handle, crumble it and set aside.
3. Pour the cooked bacon from the pan into a bowl. Add the cream cheese, peppers, parsley, spices, and salt and mix well. Refrigerate for 30-40 minutes.
4. Make 12 equal portions of the mixture and shape into balls.
5. Coat the balls in crumbled bacon and place on a plate.
6. Serve. Unused fat bombs can be placed in an airtight container in the refrigerator for 7 days.

6. Bacon and Roasted Garlic Guacamole

Cooking time: 10 minutes

Number of servings: 6

Nutritional values per serving: 1/6 portion, without serving options

- Calories – 225
- Fat – 18.74 g
- Total Carbohydrate – 11.48 g
- Digestible carbohydrate – 0 g
- Edible fibers – 6.93 g
- Protein – 6.12 g

Ingredients:

- 4 medium Hass avocados pitted, peeled, chopped
- 2 tablespoons roasted garlic
- ½ small white onion, chopped
- Freshly ground black or cayenne pepper to taste
- Salt to taste
- 2/3 medium red bell peppers, finely chopped
- 2 tablespoons fresh lime juice or to taste

- ½ teaspoon salt or to taste
- 8 slices bacon, chopped into cubes
- 2 tablespoons chopped fresh cilantro

Directions:

1. Place a pan with bacon over medium flame. Cook until crunchy. Remove the bacon with a slotted spoon and place it on a plate. Retain the bacon fat.
2. Add avocado, bell pepper, garlic, lime juice, salt, pepper, and cilantro into a bowl. Mash well.
3. Add onion and mix until well combined. Add the retained bacon fat and bacon and mix again.
4. Serve with vegetable sticks or crackers. Unused guacamole can be placed in an airtight container in the refrigerator for 6-7 days

7. Mozzarella Cheese Pockets

Cooking time: 25 minutes

Number of servings: 16

Nutritional values per serving: 1 pocket

- Calories – 271.6
- Fat – 21.7 g
- Total Carbohydrate – 3.7 g
- Digestible carbohydrate – 2.5 g
- Edible fibers – 1.2 g
- Protein – 17.1 g

Ingredients:

- 3 ½ cups grated mozzarella cheese
- 1 ½ cups almond flour
- 16 whole mozzarella cheese sticks
- 2 ounces cream cheese
- 2 large eggs
- 1 cup crushed pork rinds

Directions:

1. Add grated mozzarella cheese, cream cheese, and almond flour into a microwaveable bowl. Cook in the microwave on high for 30 seconds.
2. Remove the bowl from the microwave and add eggs. Mix well using a silicone spatula.
3. Place a sheet of parchment paper on your countertop. Place the mixture on the parchment paper. Place another sheet of parchment paper on top of the mixture. Roll with a rolling pin into the shape of a rectangle.
4. Cut into 16 equal rectangles. Wrap one rectangle around 1 mozzarella stick. Roll the rolled cheese stick around on the countertop so that the dough sticks on the cheese stick.
5. Place pork rinds on a plate. Dredge the cheese sticks in pork rinds and place them on a baking sheet. Freeze for 30 minutes.
6. Place the baking sheet in a preheated oven and bake at 400° F for about 25 minutes or until brown.

8. Cheese Chips

Cooking time: 10 minutes

Number of servings: 8

Nutritional values per serving:

- Calories – 228
- Fat – 19 g
- Total Carbohydrate – 2 g
- Digestible carbohydrate – 2 g
- Edible fibers – 0 g
- Protein – 13 g

Ingredients:

- 1 teaspoon paprika powder
- 16 ounces cheddar cheese or provolone cheese or edam cheese, shredded

Directions:

1. Place a sheet of parchment paper on a baking sheet. Place small mounds of cheese on the baking sheet. Leave sufficient gap between the mounds.

2. Garnish with paprika.
3. Bake in a preheated oven at 400° F for about 7 to 11 minutes. Keep a watch on the cheese after about 5 minutes of baking as they can get burnt.
4. Take out the baking sheet from the oven and cool completely.
5. Serve as it is or a dip of your choice.

9. Spicy Zucchini Chips

Cooking time: 45-60 minutes

Number of servings: 8

Nutritional values per serving: ¼ cup

- Calories – 54
- Fat – 3.8 g
- Total Carbohydrate – 4.6 g
- Digestible carbohydrate – 3.2 g
- Edible fibers – 1.4 g
- Protein – 1.4 g

Ingredients:

- 4 medium zucchinis or 8 baby zucchinis, cut into thin slices with a mandolin slicer
- Juice of 2 limes
- 1 teaspoon sea salt or to taste
- 2 tablespoons olive oil or coconut oil
- 1 teaspoon chili powder
- Zest of 2 limes, grated

Directions:

1. Add lime juice, lime zest, and chili powder into a bowl and stir.
2. Brush the zucchini slices with lime juice mixture and place on a lined baking sheet. Place the slices in a single layer, close to each other.
3. Season with salt. Spray some cooking spray over the zucchini slices.
4. Bake in a preheated oven at 110° F for about 45 to 60 minutes until golden brown.
5. Remove the baking sheet from the oven and cool completely.
6. Serve. Store leftovers in an airtight container.

10. Spicy Sausage Cheese Dip

Cooking time: 30-40 minutes

Number of servings: 14

Nutritional values per serving:

- Calories – 144
- Fat – 12.19 g
- Total Carbohydrate – 2.48 g
- Digestible carbohydrate – 2.47 g
- Edible fibers – 0.1 g
- Protein – 5.61 g

Ingredients:

- ½ pound hot Italian ground sausage
- 2 tablespoons thinly sliced green onion
- 8 ounces sour cream
- ½ can (from a 15 ounces can) hot diced tomatoes with habaneros
- 4 ounces cream cheese
- 4 ounces Pepper Jack cheese, chopped

Directions:

1. Place a skillet with sausage over medium flame. Cook until light brown.

2. Add tomatoes and cook for 2-3 minutes. Stir in the green onion and cook until the sausage is brown.
3. Add the remaining ingredients and stir. Cover and cook on low heat until the mixture is well incorporated. Stir occasionally.

11. Keto Mummy Dogs

Cooking time: 30 minutes

Number of servings: 8

Nutritional values per serving: 2 mummy dogs

- Calories – 759
- Fat – 67 g
- Total Carbohydrate – 7 g
- Digestible carbohydrate – 3 g
- Edible fibers – 4 g
- Protein – 29 g

Ingredients:

- 1 cup almond flour
- 1 teaspoon salt
- 5 ounces butter
- 2 eggs, for dough
- 2 eggs, beaten, for brushing on top
- 8 tablespoons coconut flour
- 2 teaspoons baking powder
- 12 ounces shredded cheese
- 2 pounds sausage links

Directions:

1. Add coconut flour, almond flour, and baking powder into a large mixing bowl. Add eggs and stir.
2. Add butter and cheese into a pan. Place the pan over low heat. Stir until the mixture is smooth. Turn off the heat.
3. Add the cheese mixture into the bowl of flour and mix until firm dough is formed.
4. Place on your countertop and divide into 2 portions. Shape each portion into a ball.
5. Roll the balls with a rolling pin into a rectangle (8 x 4 inches each). Cut each rectangle into 8 equal strips. So you should have 16 strips in all.
6. Take one strip and wrap it around one hot dog.
7. Repeat the previous step and wrap the remaining hot dogs with the dough strips.
8. Place mummies on a lined baking sheet. Brush the tops with eggs.
9. Bake in a preheated oven at 350° F for about 20 minutes or until the dough is golden brown. Switch off the oven and let the baking sheet remain in the oven for 5 minutes.
10. Serve.

12. Apple Cider Donut Bites

Cooking time: 20 minutes

Number of servings: 24

Nutritional values per serving:

- Calories – 164
- Fat – 13.71 g
- Total Carbohydrate – 4.81 g
- Digestible carbohydrate – 0 g
- Edible fibers – 2.23 g
- Protein – 6.52 g

Ingredients:

For donut bites:

- 4 cups almond flour
- ½ cup unflavored whey protein powder
- 1 teaspoon ground cinnamon
- 4 large eggs
- ½ cup melted butter
- 3 teaspoons apple extract
- 3 tablespoons apple cider vinegar
- 1 cup swerve sweetener
- 4 teaspoons baking powder

- 1 teaspoon salt

For coating:

- ½ cup swerve sweetener
- ½ cup butter, melted
- 3-4 teaspoons ground cinnamon

Directions:

1. Grease generously, a 24-count mini muffin tin with some cooking spray. If you do not have a 24-count pan, use 2 pans of 12 counts each.
2. Add all ingredients for donut bites into a bowl and whisk well.
3. Spoon the batter into the mini muffin tin.
4. Place the muffin tin in a preheated oven and bake at 325° F for about 15 to 20 minutes until light golden brown on top.
5. Take out the muffin tin from the oven and set aside to cool for a while. Remove bites from the pan and place on the wire rack to cool completely.
6. For coating: Add sweetener and cinnamon into a bowl and stir.

7. Have the melted butter ready in a bowl.
8. First dip the donut bite, one at a time, in butter. Shake to drop off excess butter. Next dredge in cinnamon mixture and place on a plate.
9. Serve. Store leftovers in an airtight container. It can last for 3-4 days.

13. Cranberry Chocolate Chip Granola Bars

Cooking time: 25 minutes

Number of servings: 8

Nutritional values per serving:

- Calories – 179
- Fat – 16.32 g
- Total Carbohydrate – 6.2 g
- Digestible carbohydrate – 3.33 g
- Edible fibers – 2.87 g
- Protein – 2.88 g

Ingredients:

- ½ cup sliced almonds
- ½ cup flaked coconut
- ¼ cup pecan halves
- 3 tablespoons dried, unsweetened, chopped cranberries
- ¼ cup sunflower seeds
- 3 tablespoons sugar-free chocolate chips
- ¼ cup butter

- ¼ cup powdered swerve sweetener
- 1 teaspoon Yacon syrup or ½ tablespoon Sukrin gold fiber syrup
- ¼ teaspoon vanilla extract

Directions:

1. Place a large sheet of parchment paper inside a small (6 x 6 inches), square baking pan such that extra paper is hanging from the sides of the pan.
2. Add coconut, pecans, almonds, and sunflower seeds into the food processor bowl. Process until crumbly.
3. Remove the mixture into a bowl. Add chocolate chips, cranberries, and salt and mix well.
4. Place a saucepan over low heat. Add butter and Yacon syrup and let it melt.
5. Add powdered swerve and whisk well. Add vanilla extract and stir. Pour into the bowl of nut mixture. Mix well.
6. Spoon the mixture into the prepared baking pan. Press the mixture in the pan.
7. Bake in a preheated oven at 300° F for about 20 to 30 minutes until light golden brown on top and golden brown around the edges.

14. Gazpacho

Cooking time: 10-15 minutes

Number of servings: 3

Nutritional values per serving:

- Calories – 529
- Fat – 50.8 g
- Total Carbohydrate – 14.3 g
- Digestible carbohydrate – 8.5 g
- Edible fibers – 5.8 g
- Protein – 7.5 g

Ingredients:

- 7 ounces ripe tomatoes, washed, remove stems
- 1 small red bell pepper, deseeded, halved
- 1 small green bell pepper, deseeded, halved
- ½ cup extra- virgin olive oil
- ½ small red onion, chopped
- 1 medium spring onion, chopped
- 1 clove garlic, peeled
- 1 tablespoon fresh lemon juice
- 2 tablespoons chopped parsley
- 2 tablespoons chopped basil

- 1 cucumber (about 3.5 ounces), peeled, chopped
- ½ teaspoon salt or to taste
- Freshly ground pepper to taste
- 3.5 ounces soft goat cheese
- 1 tablespoon apple cider vinegar or wine vinegar

Directions:

1. Place the bell peppers on a lined baking sheet, with the skin side facing up
2. Place in a preheated oven and roast at 400° F for about 20 minutes or until the skin is charred at a few places.
3. Remove from the oven and cool for a few minutes. Peel off the skin of the bell peppers and place them in a blender.
4. Add the remaining ingredients and blend well.
5. Pour into a bowl. Cover and chill until use.
6. Ladle into bowls and serve.

15. Cheese Straws

Cooking time: 30 minutes

Number of servings: 24

Nutritional values per serving: 4 cheese straws

- Calories – 209
- Fat – 18.6 g
- Total Carbohydrate – 4.5 g
- Digestible carbohydrate – 2.3 g
- Edible fibers – 2.2 g
- Protein – 6.3 g

Ingredients:

- 1 tablespoon coconut flour
- ¾ cup + 2 tablespoons almond flour
- ¼ teaspoon + 1/8 teaspoon salt
- ¼ teaspoon garlic powder
- ¼ cup butter, cut into small pieces, softened
- Yolk of 1 small egg
- ¼ teaspoon xanthan gum
- ¼ teaspoon cayenne pepper (optional)
- 2 ounces sharp cheddar cheese, grated, at room temperature

Directions:

1. Place dry ingredients into the food processor bowl. Process until well incorporated.
2. Place butter pieces at different places on the dry ingredients. Drizzle the egg yolk. Process until well incorporated and formed into a ball of dough.
3. Fit a piping bag with an open star tip. Add the dough into the piping bag.
4. Squeeze the piping bag and cut out 3-inch pieces of the cheese straws and place them on a baking sheet lined with parchment paper.
5. Place the baking sheet in a preheated oven and bake at 300° F for about 20 to 30 minutes until light golden brown. Switch off the oven and let the baking sheet remain in the oven for 5 minutes.
6. Remove from the oven and set aside to cool.
7. Once cooled, serve.

Chapter Nine: Ketogenic Dinner Recipes

1. Creamy Chicken and Mushroom Casserole

Cooking time: 10 minutes

Number of servings: 8

Nutritional values per serving:

- Calories – 400
- Fat – 29 g
- Total Carbohydrate – 5 g
- Digestible carbohydrate – 4 g
- Edible fibers – 1 g
- Protein – 27 g

Ingredients:

- 2 pounds chicken tenderloin
- 4 tablespoons butter

- 4 cloves garlic, crushed
- ¼ cup fresh thyme leaves
- 1 pound mushrooms, cut into thick slices
- 4 tablespoons olive oil
- ½ cup chopped fresh parsley
- Salt to taste
- Pepper to taste
- 1 cup heavy cream
- 1 cup chicken stock
- ½ cup sour cream

Directions:

1. Add 2 tablespoons oil and 2 tablespoons butter into a heavy skillet.
2. Place the skillet over medium flame. Let the butter melt.
3. Place chicken in the skillet and sprinkle salt and pepper. Fry until brown all over. Cook in batches if required.
4. Remove chicken and place it on a plate.
5. Add retained oil and butter into the skillet. Let the butter melt. Add mushrooms and cook until brown.

6. Add garlic, stock, and fresh herbs and mix well. Remove any browned bits that may be stuck on the bottom of the pan by scraping with a spatula.
7. Stir in the sour cream and cream and simmer until it begins to bubble slightly.
8. Add chicken and stir until well coated. Let it simmer for about 5 to 6 minutes.
9. Turn off the heat. Cover and let it sit for 10 minutes.
10. Serve. Any remaining casserole can be placed in an airtight container in the refrigerator for 5 days.

2. Skillet Chicken Florentine

Cooking time: 30 minutes

Number of servings: 2

Nutritional values per serving:

- Calories – 668
- Fat – 52 g
- Total Carbohydrate – 12 g
- Digestible carbohydrate – 8 g
- Edible fibers – 4 g
- Protein – 45 g

Ingredients:

- 2 chicken thighs, bone-in, skin on
- 6 tablespoons chicken stock
- ¼ teaspoon Himalayan pink salt
- ¼ teaspoon Italian seasoning or to taste
- ¼ teaspoon garlic powder
- Pepper to taste
- ¼ teaspoon onion powder
- 1 tablespoon avocado oil
- ½ cup heavy whipping cream
- 4 ounces cremini mushrooms, sliced

- 1 ½ cups chopped spinach
- 6 tablespoons shredded parmesan cheese

Directions:

1. Heat a cast iron skillet over medium flame. Add the oil, and once it's heated, add chicken and cook until the skin is golden brown and the chicken is nearly cooked through.
2. Take out the chicken and set aside in a bowl.
3. Pour stock and whipping cream into the skillet. Add spices and stir.
4. When the mixture begins to simmer, lower the heat and add mushrooms.
5. Cook until mushrooms are soft. Stir in parmesan and spinach. Cook until spinach wilts.
6. Add the chicken and simmer until the chicken is well cooked. Stir occasionally.
7. Serve hot.

3. Turkey Casserole

Cooking time: 25-30 minutes

Number of servings: 4

Nutritional values per serving:

- Calories – 510
- Fat – 40.98 g
- Total Carbohydrate – 8.64 g
- Digestible carbohydrate – 6.84 g
- Edible fibers – 1.8 g
- Protein – 28.72 g

Ingredients:

- 11.11 ounces turkey breast, cooked, shredded (or use leftovers)
- ¾ cup green beans
- ¼ small onion, sliced
- 4 brown mushrooms, sliced
- ½ small carrot, chopped
- 3 cloves garlic, peeled, sliced
- 2 tablespoons butter
- 1 tablespoon chopped parsley
- ½ cup broccoli florets

- ½ cup shredded cheddar cheese
- 1 tablespoon crushed pork rinds

For keto white sauce:

- 1 tablespoon butter
- ¾ cup heavy cream
- ½ teaspoon salt
- 3.5 ounces cream cheese, cut into small cubes
- ¼ cup shredded parmesan cheese
- Pepper to taste
- 1/8 teaspoon nutmeg

Directions:

1. Place a pot over medium flame. Add butter. When butter melts, add garlic, onions, and carrots and sauté for a couple of minutes.
2. Cover and cook for another 2 minutes.
3. Uncover and stir in the broccoli and mushrooms. Stir fry for a minute.
4. Cover again and cook for 2 more minutes.
5. Stir in the turkey. Remove from heat.
6. To make sauce: Place a small pot over medium flame. Add butter and cream cheese and whisk until cream cheese melts. The butter and cream cheese will not combine.

7. Stir in the heavy cream. Remove from heat. Spoon sauce over the turkey mixture and stir.
8. Spread the turkey mixture into a casserole dish.
9. Top with grated cheese. Scatter parsley and pork rinds on top.
10. Bake in a preheated oven at 300° F for about 20 to 30 minutes until golden brown.

4. Turkey with Cream-Cheese Sauce

Cooking time: 30 minutes

Number of servings: 8

Nutritional values per serving:

- Calories – 815
- Fat – 67 g
- Total Carbohydrate – 7 g
- Digestible carbohydrate – 7 g
- Edible fibers – 0 g
- Protein – 47 g

Ingredients:

- 3 pounds turkey breast
- 4 tablespoons butter
- 4 cups heavy whipping cream
- Salt to taste
- Pepper to taste
- 2 tablespoons tamari
- 14 ounces cream cheese
- 2/3 cup small capers

Directions:

1. Place a large ovenproof skillet over medium flame. Add half the butter and melt.
2. Sprinkle salt and pepper liberally over the turkey and place in the skillet.
3. Cook until brown all over.
4. Transfer the skillet into a preheated oven.
5. Roast at 350° F for about 30 minutes or the internal temperature of the meat is 165° F.
6. Remove turkey from the oven and place it on your cutting board. Cover turkey with foil loosely and let it rest for a while. When cool enough to handle, cut into slices.
7. Transfer the cooked liquid from the skillet into a saucepan. Place saucepan over medium flame. Stir in the heavy cream and cream cheese.
8. Reduce the heat to low heat and cook until thick. Add tamari, salt, and pepper and stir. Turn off the heat.
9. Place a pan over high flame. Add butter. When butter melts, add capers and cook until crisp.
10. To assemble: Place turkey slices on a large serving platter. Pour sauce over turkey. Garnish with fried capers and serve.

5. Steak Cobb Salad with Cilantro Lime Vinaigrette

Cooking time: 25 minutes

Number of servings: 2

Nutritional values per serving:

- Calories – 767
- Fat – 63 g
- Total Carbohydrate – 18 g
- Digestible carbohydrate – 8 g
- Edible fibers – 10 g
- Protein – 35 g

Ingredients:

- 2 teaspoons avocado oil
- 6 ounces grass-fed hanger steak, pat dried
- Salt to taste
- 2 cups grated cauliflower
- 2 slices bacon, minced
- 2 pasture raised eggs
- 1 avocado, peeled, pitted, chopped
- 2 cups mixed greens

- 2 cups arugula

For cilantro lime vinaigrette:

- 2 teaspoons MCT oil or Brain octane oil
- 4 tablespoons olive oil
- 1 teaspoon lime juice
- ½ teaspoon sea salt
- 2 teaspoons apple cider vinegar
- ½ cup chopped cilantro

Directions:

1. To make bacon cauliflower rice: Add bacon into a pan and cook until soft and done.
2. Stir in cauliflower rice and sauté for 4 minutes. Turn off the heat.
3. Season a generous amount of salt on either side of the steak.
4. Place a skillet over medium flame. Add the oil, and once it's heated, add the steak and cook until the brown underneath. Turn sides and cook the other side for 3-4 minutes.
5. Remove steak from the pan and place it on your cutting board.
6. When cool enough to handle, cut the steak into slices against the grain.
7. To cook eggs: Meanwhile, place a pot of water to boil. Lower the eggs into the boiling water and cook for 7 minutes.

8. Drain and immerse in plain water for a few minutes. Peel the eggs. Cut into quarters.
9. For cilantro lime dressing: Add all ingredients in a blender. Blend for about a minute or until it's all well combined.
10. Add bacon cauliflower rice, eggs, avocado, steak, and greens into a bowl and toss well.
11. Serve.

6. Crispy Sesame Beef

Cooking time: 30 minutes

Number of servings: 8

Nutritional values per serving:

- Calories – 412
- Fat – 31.3 g
- Total Carbohydrate – 8.8 g
- Digestible carbohydrate – 5 g
- Edible fibers – 3.8 g
- Protein – 24.5 g

Ingredients:

- 2 medium daikon radishes (about 1.5 pound in all)
- 2 tablespoons coconut flour
- 2 tablespoons coconut oil
- 2 teaspoons sesame oil
- 3 tablespoons rice vinegar
- 1 teaspoon red pepper flakes
- 1 medium jalapeno pepper, thinly sliced
- 1 medium red pepper, sliced into thin strips
- 2 medium green onions, chopped

- 2 teaspoons ginger, minced
- 2 cloves garlic, minced
- 2 pounds rib-eye steak, sliced into ¼" strips
- 1 teaspoon guar gum
- ½ cup soy sauce or tamari
- 2 teaspoons oyster sauce
- 2 teaspoons Sriracha
- 2 tablespoons sesame seeds, toasted
- 10 drops Liquid Stevia (optional)
- Oil for frying, as required

Directions:

1. Make noodles of the daikon radish using a spiralizer or julienne peeler.
2. Soak the noodles in a bowl of cold water for about 20-25 minutes. Drain in a colander.
3. Place a large frying pan or wok over high flame. Add the oil, and once it's heated add ginger, garlic, and red pepper. Sauté until it gets fragrant. Add sesame seeds and sauté for a couple of minutes.
4. Add soy sauce, oyster sauce, sesame oil, vinegar, Sriracha, and stevia. Mix well and let it cook for a couple of minutes. Remove from heat.

5. Meanwhile, place a deep pan over medium flame. Pour enough oil into the pan so that it covers at least an inch in height from the bottom of the pan.
6. When the temperature of the oil is nearly 325° F, add beef strips in batches and cook until brown all over.
7. Remove the strips and place them on paper towels.
8. Place the wok over medium flame. Add the crispy beef strips and mixture of sauces and cook for a couple of minutes.
9. To serve: Divide equally the daikon noodles and place on individual serving plates. Top with a few crispy beef strips along with sauce and serve.

7. Fat Bomb Pork Chops

Cooking time: 30 minutes

Number of servings: 6

Nutritional values per serving:

- Calories – 1121
- Fat – 104 g
- Total Carbohydrate – 9 g
- Digestible carbohydrate – 8 g
- Edible fibers – 1 g
- Protein – 35 g

Ingredients:

- 2 medium yellow onions, sliced
- 1 cup oil
- 2 teaspoons garlic powder
- 2 cups keto-friendly mayonnaise
- 2 packages (8 ounces each) brown mushrooms, sliced
- 6 medium boneless pork chops
- 2 teaspoons ground nutmeg
- 2 tablespoons balsamic vinegar

Directions:

1. Heat a large skillet over low heat. Add the oil, and once it's heated, add onions and mushrooms and cook until onions are translucent.
2. Move the vegetables to one of the sides of the skillet.
3. Place the pork chops in the center of the skillet. Season both the sides of the pork with nutmeg and garlic powder. Cook until the pork is cooked inside and brown on the outside.
4. Remove pork and place it on a plate.
5. Move the onion and mushrooms to the center of the pan. Add mayonnaise and vinegar and stir until well combined. If you find the sauce very thick, add a little water or broth and stir.
6. Spoon the sauce over the chops and serve.

8. Italian Sausage Stuffed Mushrooms

Cooking time: 20 minutes

Number of servings: 8

Nutritional values per serving:

- Calories – 578
- Fat – 47 g
- Total Carbohydrate – 12 g
- Digestible carbohydrate – 10 g
- Edible fibers – 2 g
- Protein – 26 g

Ingredients:

- 8 Jumbo Portobello mushroom caps, remove stems
- 2 cups shredded Pepper Jack cheese
- ½ cup chopped fresh basil
- Salt to taste
- 2 pounds Italian sausage
- 3 cups keto-friendly marinara sauce
- 4 cloves garlic, minced

- Pepper to taste

Directions:

1. Place the mushroom caps on a lined baking sheet, with the stem part facing up.
2. Place the baking sheet in a preheated oven and bake at 375° F for about 15 to 20 minutes or until slightly soft.
3. In the meantime, place a skillet over medium-high flame. Place sausage in the pan and cook until brown. Break it simultaneously as it cooks.
4. Lower the heat to medium flame. Stir in the garlic and cook until aromatic.
5. Add the remaining ingredients except cheese and mix well. Discard any cooked liquid from the mushrooms.
6. Stuff the sausage mixture into the mushroom caps. Sprinkle cheese on top.
7. Broil in an oven until cheese melts and is browned as per your desire.

9. Lamb Chops with Herb Butter

Cooking time: 10 minutes

Number of servings: 2

Nutritional values per serving:

- Calories – 723
- Fat – 62 g
- Total Carbohydrate – 0.3 g
- Digestible carbohydrate – 0.3 g,
- Edible fibers – 0 g
- Protein – 43 g

Ingredients:

- 4 lamb chops, at room temperature
- ½ tablespoon olive oil
- ½ tablespoon butter
- Salt to taste
- Pepper to taste
- Lemon wedges, to serve
- 2 ounces herb butter, to serve

Directions:

1. Sprinkle salt and pepper over the lamb chops.
2. Place a skillet over medium flame. Heat oil and butter in the skillet and when butter melts, add lamb chops and cook to the desired doneness.
3. Remove from the pan and place on individual serving plates. Top with butter and serve with lemon wedges.

10. Lamb Burgers

Cooking time: 15 minutes

Number of servings: 5

Nutritional values per serving:

- Calories – 397
- Fat – 33 g
- Total Carbohydrate – 1 g
- Digestible carbohydrate – 1 g
- Edible fibers – 0 g
- Protein – 22 g

Ingredients:

For lamb and halloumi burgers:

- 1 pound ground lamb
- 1 egg
- ½ tablespoons finely chopped parsley
- Salt to taste
- Pepper to taste
- 4.5 ounces halloumi cheese, grated
- 1 teaspoon ground cumin
- ½ teaspoon finely chopped rosemary

For cucumber cream:

- 4 ounces sour cream
- ½ teaspoon ground cumin
- Pepper to taste
- Salt to taste
- 1.75 ounces cucumber, deseeded, finely diced

Directions:

1. For the burgers: Add ground lamb, egg, parsley, seasonings, cheese, cumin, and rosemary into a bowl and mix well.
2. Make 5 equal portions of the lamb mixture and shape into patties.
3. Keep a grill pan over medium-high flame. When the pan heats, cook the burgers in batches for 5 to 8 minutes or to the desired doneness. You can also grill the burgers on a preheated grill.
4. Meanwhile, add all ingredients for cucumber cream into a bowl and mix well.
5. Serve burgers with cucumber cream.

11. Fish in Lemon Butter Caper Sauce

Cooking time: 5 minutes

Number of servings: 4

Nutritional values per serving:

- Calories – 392
- Fat – 32 g
- Total Carbohydrate – 9 g
- Digestible carbohydrate – 7 g
- Edible fibers – 2 g
- Protein – 18 g

Ingredients:

- 1.1 pounds fish fillets
- 1 ounce capers
- 2 cloves garlic, minced
- 2 tablespoons olive oil
- Salt to taste
- Pepper to taste
- 5.6 ounces butter
- 1 medium onion, chopped

- 1 tablespoon chopped parsley
- Lemon juice to drizzle

Directions:

1. Place a nonstick pan with oil over medium flame.
2. Place fish in the pan and sprinkle salt and pepper over it. Cook until the fish is cooked.
3. Transfer the fish into a bowl.
4. Place onions in the same pan cook until translucent.
5. Stir in a little of the butter and let it melt. Add garlic and cook until fragrant.
6. Stir in the capers. Break it with a spatula. Add a little more butter and parsley and stir until butter melts. Remove from heat.
7. Add remaining butter and lemon juice and stir.
8. Spoon the sauce over the fish and serve.

12. Creamy Garlic Shrimp

Cooking time: 10 minutes

Number of servings: 8

Nutritional values per serving: Without serving options

- Calories – 488
- Fat – 44 g
- Total Carbohydrate – 4 g
- Digestible carbohydrate – 4 g
- Edible fibers – 0 g
- Protein – 30 g

Ingredients:

- 2 tablespoons olive oil
- Salt to taste
- Pepper to taste
- 12 cloves garlic, minced
- 3 cups reduced fat cream
- ¼ cup chopped parsley
- 2 pounds shrimp
- 4 tablespoons unsalted butter
- 1 cup chicken broth

- 1 cup freshly grated parmesan cheese

Directions:

1. Place a large skillet with oil over medium-high flame and heat the oil.
2. Sprinkle salt and pepper over the shrimp and place in the skillet. Cook for a couple of minutes. Turn over the shrimp and cook for a couple of minutes or until pink. Remove the shrimp from the pan and place in a bowl.
3. Add butter into the skillet. When butter melts, add garlic and stir fry for a few seconds until aromatic.
4. Stir in the broth and scrape the bottom of the pan using the spatula to loosen any brown bits that may be stuck.
5. Once it starts to boil, lower the heat to medium-low. Stir in the cream. Add salt and pepper to taste.
6. When it begins to bubble, add parmesan cheese and let it cook for a minute.
7. Add shrimp and parsley and stir until shrimp is well coated with the sauce. Turn off the heat.
8. Serve over keto-friendly pasta or cauliflower rice.

13. Spicy Almond Tofu

Cooking time: 15 minutes

Number of servings: 4

Nutritional values per serving: Without serving options

- Calories – 400
- Fat – 29 g
- Total Carbohydrate – 10 g
- Digestible carbohydrate – 5 g
- Edible fibers – 5 g
- Protein – 24 g

Ingredients:

- 1 teaspoon garlic powder
- ½ cup water
- 4 teaspoons sesame oil
- 8 tablespoons green chili sauce
- 1 teaspoon Himalayan pink salt or more to taste
- 1 teaspoon paprika
- 1 teaspoon onion powder

- 8 tablespoons liquid aminos
- ½ teaspoon chili flakes
- 4 packages firm tofu or extra- firm tofu, pressed of excess moisture, cubed
- 4 tablespoons coconut oil
- 4 tablespoons sesame seeds, divided
- 1 teaspoon pepper to taste
- ½ cup sliced almonds

Directions:

1. Heat a skillet with coconut oil over medium flame. Once the oil gets heated, add tofu and cook until golden brown on all the sides and is crisp.
2. Add almonds and cook for a couple of minutes. Retain ½ tablespoon sesame seeds and sesame oil and add the rest of the ingredients. Cook until all the liquid in the pan is absorbed.
3. Serving over steamed broccoli or any other steamed vegetables is a good option. Drizzle sesame oil over tofu. Sprinkle remaining sesame seeds on top and serve.

14. Vegan Dinner Bowl

Cooking time: 30 minutes

Number of servings: 2

Nutritional values per serving:

- Calories – 423
- Fat – 27 g
- Total Carbohydrate – 30 g
- Digestible carbohydrate – 16 g
- Edible fibers – 14 g
- Protein – 23 g

Ingredients:

For baked tofu:

- ½ package firm tofu, pressed of excess moisture
- ½ teaspoon garlic powder
- Pepper to taste
- 1 tablespoon soy sauce or tamari
- ½ tablespoon arrowroot powder

For almond butter sauce:

- 2 tablespoons almond butter or sunflower seed butter

- ½ tablespoon unseasoned rice wine vinegar
- 2 tablespoons unsweetened almond or coconut milk
- Salt to taste
- Pepper to taste
- 1 tablespoon soy sauce or tamari
- 1 teaspoon sriracha sauce
- 5 drops liquid stevia

For cabbage rice:

- ¼ cup chopped green onions
- ½ small green cabbage, cut into chunks
- 2 cloves garlic, minced
- ½ teaspoon coconut oil
- ¼ cup chopped cilantro

For bowl:

- 1 small avocado, peeled, pitted, chopped
- 2 cups chopped kale, steamed
- 2 cups broccoli florets, steamed

Directions:

1. Add all ingredients for baked tofu into a bowl and toss well. Place on a lined baking sheet and spread it evenly.

2. Place the baking sheet in a preheated oven and bake at 375º F for about 15 to 20 minutes or until brown.
3. To make cabbage rice: Place cabbage in the food processor bowl and process until it is rice-like in texture.
4. Place a skillet over high flame. Add cabbage and remaining ingredients for cabbage rice and mix well. Do not stir for about 2-3 minutes. Stir again. Repeat this a few times until the cabbage is slightly brown.
5. For almond butter sauce: Add almond butter, vinegar, milk, pepper, soy sauce, salt, sriracha, and stevia into a bowl and whisk well.
6. To make bowls: Divide cabbage rice among 2 bowls. Layer with kale and broccoli, followed by avocado and tofu. Drizzle sauce on top and serve.

15. Cheese Quiche Stuffed Peppers

Cooking time: 45 minutes

Number of servings: 2

Nutritional values per serving:

- Calories – 245.5
- Fat – 16.28 g
- Total Carbohydrate – 7.1 g
- Digestible carbohydrate – 5.97 g
- Edible fibers – 1.13 g
- Protein – 17.84 g

Ingredients:

- 1 medium bell pepper, halved lengthwise, deseeded
- ¼ cup ricotta cheese
- ¼ cup grated parmesan cheese + 1 tablespoon to garnish
- 1/8 teaspoon dried parsley
- 2 large eggs
- ¼ cup shredded mozzarella cheese
- ½ teaspoon garlic powder
- A handful baby spinach leaves, chopped

Directions:

1. Add eggs, parsley, garlic powder, parmesan cheese, mozzarella cheese, and ricotta cheese into the food processor bowl and process until well combined.
2. Fill this mixture into the bell pepper halves. Do not fill up to the top.
3. Place spinach leaves on top and press the leaves lightly into the filling.
4. Place a sheet of foil on top of the bell pepper halves.
5. Place the baking sheet in a preheated oven and bake at 375° F for about 30 to 40 minutes or until the eggs are cooked.
6. Uncover and broil for a couple of minutes until light brown on top.

Chapter Ten: Ketogenic Dessert Recipes

1. Chocolate Frosty

Cooking time: 10 minutes

Number of servings: 8

Nutritional values per serving:

- Calories – 241
- Fat – 25 g
- Total Carbohydrate – 4 g
- Digestible carbohydrate – 3 g
- Edible fibers – 1 g
- Protein – 3 g

Ingredients:

- 2 cups heavy whipping cream
- 4 tablespoons unsweetened cocoa powder
- 2 teaspoons vanilla extract
- 2 tablespoons almond butter

- 1 teaspoon liquid stevia

Directions:

1. Add cream cocoa, vanilla almond butter, and stevia into a bowl. Beat with an electric hand mixer until peaks are stiff.
2. Freeze for about 60 minutes. Spoon into a piping bag. Pipe into 8 dessert bowls.

2. Strawberry Mousse

Cooking time: 20 minutes

Number of servings: 8

Nutritional values per serving:

- Calories – 253
- Fat – 25.7 g
- Total Carbohydrate – 4.5 g
- Digestible carbohydrate – 3.7 g
- Edible fibers – 0.8 g
- Protein – 2.5 g

Ingredients:

- 3 ½ cups coconut cream
- 2 cups, sliced strawberries
- 2-4 teaspoons swerve or erythritol

Directions:

1. Add coconut cream into a bowl. Whisk with an electric hand mixer until creamy.

2. Retain a few strawberry slices. Add the rest of strawberries and swerve into another bowl. Blend it well until it becomes smooth.
3. Add strawberry mixture into the bowl of coconut cream and fold gently.
4. Divide the mousse into 8 small glasses.
5. Garnish with strawberry slices.
6. Chill for a while and serve.

3. Italian Cream Chaffle Cake

Cooking time: 3 – 4 minutes per chaffle

Number of servings: 4

Nutritional values per serving: 1 chaffle

- Calories – 127
- Fat – 9.7 g
- Total Carbohydrate – 5.5 g
- Digestible carbohydrate – 4.2 g
- Edible fibers – 1.3 g
- Protein – 5.3 g

Ingredients:

For chaffles:

- 2 ounces cream cheese, softened
- ½ tablespoon butter, melted
- ¼ teaspoon ground cinnamon
- ½ tablespoon almond flour
- 2 tablespoons coconut flour
- ½ tablespoon shredded, unsweetened coconut
- 2 eggs
- ½ teaspoon vanilla extract

- ½ tablespoon monk fruit sweetener or erythritol
- ¾ teaspoon baking powder
- ½ tablespoon chopped walnuts

For Italian cream frosting:

- 1 ounce cream cheese, softened
- 1 tablespoon monk fruit sweetener or any other keto-friendly sweetener of your choice
- 1 tablespoon butter
- ¼ teaspoon vanilla

Directions:

1. Cool the melted butter to room temperature.
2. Add all ingredients except walnuts and shredded coconut into a blender and blend until it becomes smooth.
3. Pour into a bowl.
4. Add walnuts and shredded coconut and stir.
5. Pour ¼ of the batter into a preheated mini waffle maker. Set the timer for 2-3 minutes. Close the lid of the waffle maker.

6. Take out the chaffle and place it on a plate.
7. Repeat the previous two steps and make the remaining chaffles. Let the chaffles cool completely.
8. To make frosting: Add cream cheese, sweetener, butter, and vanilla into a bowl and whisk until it becomes smooth and well combined.
9. Place the chaffles on a large serving platter. Spread the frosting over the chaffles and serve.

4. Avocado Popsicle with Coconut & Lime

Cooking time: 10 minutes

Number of servings: 12

Nutritional values per serving: 1 Popsicle

- Calories – 219
- Fat – 21 g
- Total Carbohydrate – 8 g
- Digestible carbohydrate – 4 g
- Edible fibers – 4 g
- Protein – 2 g

Ingredients:

- 3 tablespoons lime juice
- 6 tablespoons erythritol or granular swerve sweetener
- 2 ¼ cups coconut milk
- 3 avocados, peeled, pitted, chopped

Directions:

1. Add avocado, lime juice, sweetener, and coconut milk into a blender and blend it until it becomes smooth.
2. Divide into 9 Popsicle molds. Insert the Popsicle sticks and freeze until firm.
3. To serve: Dip the Popsicle molds in warm water for a few seconds. Remove from the molds and serve.

5. Chocolate Cheesecake Fat Bombs

Cooking time: 40 minutes

Number of servings: 6

Nutritional values per serving:

- Calories – 333
- Fat – 32 g
- Total Carbohydrate – 8 g
- Digestible carbohydrate – 4 g
- Edible fibers – 4 g
- Protein – 4 g

Ingredients:

- 4 ounces cream cheese, softened
- 2 tablespoons powdered swerve
- 2 tablespoons almond butter
- 4 tablespoons grass fed butter
- 2 tablespoon unsweetened cocoa powder

Directions:

1. Add cream cheese into a mixing bowl. Mix with an electric mixer, on medium speed until fluffy. Scrape the sides with a spatula.
2. Add the remaining ingredients and beat until well incorporated.
3. Divide the mixture into 6 equal portions and shape into balls. Place on a plate.
4. Chill until use.

6. Blackberry & Lemon Mini Tarts

Cooking time: 20 minutes

Number of servings: 20

Nutritional values per serving:

- Calories – 178
- Fat – 16.2 g
- Total Carbohydrate – 5.9 g
- Digestible carbohydrate – 2.8 g
- Edible fibers – 3.1 g
- Protein – 4.4 g

Ingredients:

For crust:

- 2 cups macadamia nuts
- 2 large eggs
- 1 ½ cups powdered, desiccated coconut

For filling:

- 2 cups coconut milk
- 2 tablespoons grated lemon zest
- 20-30 drops stevia (optional)
- 5-6 tablespoons water

- Juice of a lemon
- ½ cup erythritol or swerve, powdered
- 3 tablespoons gelatin powder

For topping:

- 2 cups blackberries, fresh or frozen

Directions:

1. Stir together gelatin and water in another bowl and add into the saucepan with coconut milk mixture. Stir until well combined. Let it cool for a while. Refrigerate for 30 minutes.
2. It will be thick. The mixture should jiggle but should not be firm.
3. To make crust: Add macadamia nuts and coconut into the food processor bowl. Process until the texture you desire is achieved. Add eggs. Mix well.
4. Line 20 mini muffin molds with paper cup liners. Divide the nut mixture into the muffin pan.
5. Place the muffin pan in a preheated oven and bake at 400° F for 5-7 minutes.
6. When done, cool completely. Remove tarts from the molds. Place on a tray. Spoon the filling on the crusts. Place 3 blackberries on each cheesecake.
7. Chill until use.

7. Keto Brown Butter Pralines

Cooking time: 11 minutes

Number of servings: 5

Nutritional values per serving:

- Calories – 338
- Fat – 36 g
- Total Carbohydrate – 3 g
- Digestible carbohydrate – 1 g
- Edible fibers – 2 g
- Protein – 2 g

Ingredients:

- 8 tablespoons salted butter
- 1/3 cup granular sweetener
- 1 cup chopped pecans
- 1/3 cup heavy cream
- ¼ teaspoon xanthan gum
- Maldon salt to garnish (optional)

Directions:

1. Place a saucepan with butter over medium-high flame. In a few minutes, butter will become brown. Stir frequently.
2. Add cream, sweetener, and xanthan gum and whisk until well combined. Turn off the heat.
3. Add pecans and mix well. Cool for a few minutes and transfer the saucepan into the refrigerator. Let it chill for an hour.
4. Divide the mixture into 5 equal portions and shape into balls. Flatten them and place them on a tray lined with parchment paper.
5. Garnish with maldon salt if using. Chill until firm.
6. Transfer into an airtight container and refrigerate until use.

8. Chewy Chocolate Chip Cookies

Cooking time: 20 minutes

Number of servings: 30

Nutritional values per serving: 1 cookie

- Calories – 120
- Fat – 11 g
- Total Carbohydrate – 4.5 g
- Digestible carbohydrate – 1.5 g
- Edible fibers – 3 g
- Protein – 4 g

Ingredients:

For dry ingredients:

- ¾ cup coconut flour
- 2 cups almond flour
- 2 tablespoons xanthan gum
- ½ teaspoon baking powder
- 1 teaspoon baking soda
- ½ teaspoon salt

For wet ingredients:

- ¾ cup unsalted butter, at room temperature
- 7 tablespoons truvia
- 2 teaspoons vanilla extract
- ½ cup stevia sweetened chocolate chips
- 1 teaspoon blackstrap molasses (optional)
- 4 eggs
- 13 tablespoons splenda

Directions:

1. Combine the dry ingredients into a mixing bowl.
2. Add butter, truvia, blackstrap molasses, vanilla, and splenda into another bowl. Beat with an electric hand mixer until creamy.
3. Beat in the eggs. Add the beaten wet ingredients into the bowl of dry ingredients and mix until dough is formed.
4. Add chocolate chips and fold gently. Cover the bowl and chill for about 20 to 25 minutes.
5. Divide the dough into 30 equal portions and shape into balls. Flatten the dough to shape like cookies and place on a greased baking sheet. Leave a gap of at least an inch between 2 cookies.

6. Place the baking sheet in a preheated oven and bake at 350° F for 8 to 9 minutes or until the underside is light brown.
7. Let the cookies cool for 15 minutes on the baking sheet itself.
8. Remove the cookies and place them on a tray to cool completely.
9. Transfer into an airtight container.

9. Cheesecake Fluff

Cooking time: 10 minutes

Number of servings: 12

Nutritional values per serving: Without toppings

- Calories – 258
- Fat – 27 g
- Total Carbohydrate – 4 g
- Digestible carbohydrate – 4 g
- Edible fibers – 0 g
- Protein – 4 g

Ingredients:

- 2 cups heavy whipping cream
- Zest of 2 lemons, grated
- 2 bricks (8 ounces each) cream cheese, softened
- 1 cup granular swerve

Directions:

1. Beat cream in a mixing bowl with an electric hand mixer until stiff peaks are visible. Keep it aside.

2. Add cream cheese, sweetener, and lemon zest into another mixing bowl. Beat until creamy.
3. Transfer the whipped cream into the bowl of cream cheese. Mix gently using a spatula.
4. Whip with an electric hand mixer until it becomes smooth.
5. Divide into 12 dessert bowls. Serve with keto-friendly toppings of your choice.

10. Avocado Brownies

Cooking time: 40 minutes

Number of servings: 24

Nutritional values per serving:

- Calories – 158
- Fat – 14.29 g
- Total Carbohydrate – 9 g
- Digestible carbohydrate – 5.16 g
- Edible fibers – 6.6 g
- Protein – 3.84 g

Ingredients:

Wet ingredients:

- 4 avocados (1.1 pounds in all), peeled, pitted, chopped
- ½ cup cocoa powder
- 6 tablespoons refined coconut oil
- 7 ounces keto-friendly dark chocolate, melted
- 1 teaspoon vanilla extract
- 2 teaspoons stevia powder
- 4 eggs

For dry ingredients:

- 6.3 ounces blanched almond flour
- ½ cup erythritol
- 2 teaspoons baking powder
- ½ teaspoon baking soda
- ½ teaspoon salt

Directions:

1. Process the avocados in the food processor bowl until creamy.
2. Add the remaining wet ingredients one at a time and pulse well each time until well combined.
3. Add all the dry ingredients into another bowl and stir until well incorporated. Add into the food processor bowl and process until well incorporated.
4. Line a large baking dish with parchment paper. Spoon the batter into the baking dish.
5. Place the baking dish in a preheated oven and bake at 350° F for about 35-40 minutes.
6. Let the brownies cool completely on a cooling rack. Cut into 24 pieces of the same size and serve.
7. Place leftovers in an airtight container, in the refrigerator for up to 4 days.

11. Keto Ice Cream

Cooking time: 20 minutes

Number of servings: 10

Nutritional values per serving:

- Calories – 184
- Fat – 19.1 g
- Total Carbohydrate – 4.4 g
- Digestible carbohydrate – 2.6 g
- Edible fibers – 1.8 g
- Protein – 1.8 g

Ingredients:

- 4 cups canned, full fat coconut milk
- 3 teaspoons pure vanilla extract
- ¼ teaspoon salt
- 2/3 cup xylitol or erythritol or any other keto-friendly sweetener of your choice

Directions:

1. Combine all ingredients and add into a bowl and stir until well-combined and the sweetener dissolves completely.

2. Pour the mixture into an ice cream maker. Make the ice cream following the manufacturer's instructions. Scoop into bowls and serve, if eating immediately. If you want to serve later, spoon the ice cream into a freezer safe container and freeze until firm. Remove from the freezer 10 minutes before serving. Scoop into bowls and serve.
3. If you do not have an ice cream machine, pour the mixture into ice cube trays. Freeze until firm.
4. To serve: Remove the frozen ice cream cubes and place them in a food processor. Process until soft serve consistency.
5. Scoop into bowls and serve.

12. Chocolate Pudding

Cooking time: 15-20 minutes

Number of servings: 8

Nutritional values per serving:

- Calories – 247
- Fat – 24 g
- Total Carbohydrate – 5 g
- Digestible carbohydrate – 5 g
- Edible fibers – 3 g
- Protein – 2 g

Ingredients:

- 3 teaspoons vanilla extract
- 3 teaspoons xanthan gum
- 3 extra-large eggs
- ¾ cup unsweetened cocoa powder
- 1 cup truvia
- 3 cups unsweetened almond milk
- 3 cups heavy cream
- Whipped cream to serve

Directions:

1. Add vanilla, xanthan gum, eggs, cocoa, truvia, milk, and heavy cream into a saucepan and whisk until well combined.
2. Keep the saucepan over medium-low heat. Stir frequently until the mixture is thickened. Do not boil it. It should only be bubbling all the while. Add more xanthan gum if the pudding is not thick enough to coat the behind of a spoon. Turn off the heat. Add vanilla and stir until well incorporated.
3. Divide into 12 dessert bowls. Cover each bowl with cling wrap and chill until use.
4. Top with whipped cream and serve.

13. Mini Cinnamon Roll Cheesecakes

Cooking time: 30 minutes

Number of servings: 12

Nutritional values per serving: 1 mini cheesecake

- Calories – 237
- Fat – 20.59 g
- Total Carbohydrate – 4.63 g
- Digestible carbohydrate – 2.94 g
- Edible fibers – 1.69 g
- Protein – 4.63 g

Ingredients:

For crust:

- 1 cup almond flour
- 1 teaspoon ground cinnamon
- 4 tablespoons swerve sweetener
- 4 tablespoons melted butter

For cheesecake filling:

- 12 ounces cream cheese, softened
- ½ cup sour cream
- 2 large eggs
- 10 tablespoons swerve sweetener, divided
- 1 teaspoon vanilla extract
- 4 teaspoons ground cinnamon

For frosting:

- 2 tablespoons butter, softened
- ½ teaspoon vanilla extract
- 6 tablespoons confectioners swerve sweetener
- 4 teaspoons heavy cream

Directions:

1. To make crust: Place disposable liners in each of the wells of a 12 count muffin pan.
2. Add almond flour, cinnamon, and sweetener and whisk until well-combined. Add butter and stir until they stick together.
3. Divide equally and spoon into the muffin pan. Press it well with the back of a spoon so that it settles down.

4. Place the muffin pan in a preheated oven at 325° F for about 7-8 minutes.
5. To make cheesecake filling: Lower the temperature of the oven to 300° F.
6. Add cream cheese and 6 tablespoons swerve into a mixing bowl. Beat with an electric hand mixer until it becomes smooth.
7. Add sour cream, eggs, and vanilla and beat well.
8. To make cinnamon sugar: Add 4 tablespoons sweetener and cinnamon into a bowl and stir.
9. Divide the filling among the muffin cups. Sprinkle cinnamon sugar over the filling.
10. Place in the oven and bake for about 15 minutes or until the edges are set and the center jiggles a bit. Switch off the oven and let the muffin pan remain in the oven for another 5 minutes.
11. Remove the muffin pan from the oven and set aside until it cools. Remove the cheesecake crusts from the pan and place on a tray.
12. Place the cheesecakes in the refrigerator until set.

13. To make frosting: Add butter and swerve confectioners into a mixing bowl. Beat with an electric hand mixer until creamy. Add vanilla and heavy cream and beat until creamy.
14. Spoon the frosting into a piping bag. Pipe onto the cheesecakes and serve.

14. Almond Flour Blondies

Cooking time: 16-17 minutes

Number of servings: 8

Nutritional values per serving:

- Calories – 84
- Fat – 0 g
- Total Carbohydrate – 3.5 g
- Digestible carbohydrate – 1.7 g
- Edible fibers – 1.8 g
- Protein – 3.1 g

Ingredients:

- 1 tablespoon coconut flour
- 1 cup blanched almond flour
- ½ teaspoon baking powder
- 3 tablespoons swerve brown sugar substitute
- 1/8 teaspoon fine sea salt
- 2 tablespoons water

Directions:

1. Combine all ingredients into a mixing bowl and stir until well incorporated.
2. Pour batter into a small (8 x 8 inches), lined baking dish.
3. Place the baking dish in a preheated oven and bake at 350° F for about 14-17 minutes or until brown on top.
4. Take out the baking dish from the oven and let it cool to room temperature.
5. Cut into 12 equal squares and serve.
6. Blondie's can be stored in an airtight container. It can last for 2 days at room temperature.

15. Magical Frozen Fudge Pops

Cooking time: 10-12 minutes

Number of servings: 8

Nutritional values per serving: 1 pop

- Calories – 303
- Fat – 26 g
- Total Carbohydrate – 6 g
- Digestible carbohydrate – 5 g
- Edible fibers – 1 g
- Protein – 11 g

Ingredients:

- 2 tablespoons unsweetened cocoa powder
- 4 tablespoons Brain octane oil
- 2 cups coconut cream
- 4 pasture raised egg yolks
- Liquid stevia to taste
- ¼ teaspoon salt
- 2 teaspoons vanilla powder
- 2 tablespoons cacao butter
- 4 tablespoons collagelatin

Directions:

1. Add Brain octane oil, cacao butter, salt, collagelatin, cocoa, vanilla, and coconut cream into a saucepan.
2. Place the saucepan over low heat. When it begins to bubble and is well-incorporated, turn off the heat. Stir frequently.
3. Allow it to cool completely. Transfer into a blender. Also add yolks and sweetener into the blender and blend it until it's all well incorporated.
4. Pour into Popsicle molds. Insert the Popsicle sticks in the molds and freeze until firm.
5. Remove from the freezer before serving. Dip the molds in a bowl of warm water for 15-20 seconds. Remove from the molds and serve.

Chapter Eleven: Two Week Diet Plan

Now that you have mastered cooking keto recipes, here is a sample meal plan for 2 weeks. This 15-days meal plan can be altered in any manner as you please. You don't have to eat all 5 meals if you aren't up to it; this is just a sample plan to make your keto journey easy so you are not confused about what to eat.

Day 1

Breakfast – Breakfast Sandwich

Lunch – Grilled Chicken Salad

Snack - Cheddar Cheese and Bacon Balls

Dinner – Creamy Chicken and Mushroom Casserole

Dessert - Avocado Popsicle with Coconut & Lime

Breakfast – Brussels Sprouts Casserole Au Gratin with Bacon

Lunch – Curried Cabbage Coconut Salad

Snack - Smoked Salmon Appetizer

Dinner – Skillet Chicken Florentine

Dessert - Blackberry & Lemon Mini Tarts

Day 3

Breakfast – Taco Breakfast Skillet

Lunch – Keto "Potato" Salad

Snack - Chocolate Cranberry Muffins

Dinner – Turkey Casserole

Dessert - Chocolate Cheesecake Fat Bombs

Day 4

Breakfast – Keto Oatmeal

Lunch – Turmeric & Cauliflower Soup

Snack - Pina Colada Fat Bombs

Dinner – Turkey with Cream-Cheese Sauce

Dessert - Mini Cinnamon Roll Cheesecakes

Day 5

Breakfast – Keto Dutch Baby

Lunch – Roasted Tomato Soup

Snack - Jalapeño Popper Fat Bombs

Dinner – Steak Cobb Salad with Cilantro Lime Vinaigrette

Dessert - Keto Brown Butter Pralines

Day 6

Breakfast – Mini Pancake Donuts

Lunch – One Pot Creamy Meatball Soup

Snack - Bacon and Roasted Garlic Guacamole

Dinner – Crispy Sesame Beef

Dessert - Avocado Brownies

Day 7

Breakfast – Breakfast Bowl

Lunch – Skillet Pizza

Snack - Mozzarella Cheese Pockets

Dinner – Fat Bomb Pork Chops

Dessert - Cheesecake Fluff

Day 8

Breakfast – Keto Breakfast "Potatoes"

Lunch – Zucchini Boats

Snack - Cheese Chips

Dinner – Italian Sausage Stuffed Mushrooms

Dessert - Chocolate Pudding

Day 9

Breakfast – Tomatoes and Cheese Frittata

Lunch – Chicken Stir-Fry with Shirataki Noodles

Snack - Spicy Zucchini Chips

Dinner – Lamb Chops with Herb Butter

Dessert - Keto Ice Cream

Day 10

Breakfast – Bacon and Zucchini Hash

Lunch – Salmon Pie

Snack - Spicy Sausage Cheese Dip

Dinner – Lamb Burgers

Dessert - Chewy Chocolate Chip Cookies

Day 11

Breakfast – Cinnamon Swirl Bread

Lunch – Salmon-Filled Avocados

Snack - Keto Mummy Dogs

Dinner – Fish in Lemon Butter Caper Sauce

Dessert - Strawberry Mousse

Day 12

Breakfast – Blueberry Pancakes

Lunch – Bacon Avocado Sandwich

Snack - Apple Cider Donut Bites

Dinner – Creamy Garlic Shrimp

Dessert - Almond Flour Blondies

Day 13

Breakfast – Triple Berry Avocado Breakfast Smoothie

Lunch – Coconut Lime Noodles with Chili Tamari Tofu

Snack - Cranberry Chocolate Chip Granola Bars

Dinner – Spicy Almond Tofu

Dessert - Italian Cream Chaffle Cake

Day 14

Breakfast – Chocolate Peanut Butter Smoothie

Lunch – Quesadillas

Snack - Gazpacho

Dinner – Vegan Dinner Bowl

Dessert - Magical Frozen Fudge Pops

Day 15

Breakfast – Mushroom Omelet

Lunch – Keto Burgers

Snack - Cheese Straws

Dinner – 3 Cheese Quiche Stuffed Peppers

Dessert - Chocolate Frosty

Conclusion

I want to thank you once again for purchasing this book. I hope you found it to be an informative and enjoyable read.

Now that you have gone through all the information given about the ketogenic diet, it probably doesn't sound intimidating or difficult. The ketogenic diet is so much more than a basic diet. Instead, it is a healthier approach to life. By following this diet, you can easily attain your weight loss and fitness objectives while improving your overall health.

In this book, you were given all the information you require about the keto diet. From understanding the different variations it offers to a food list, you can use the helpful tips given to get started with this wonderful diet immediately. By increasing your intake of naturally fatty foods while limiting or avoiding carbs altogether, you will feel more energized. Start using the different recipes given in this book to cook delicious and healthy meals within no time. All that you need to do is start stocking up on the required groceries, select a recipe, and get cooking.

This diet will make you feel more energetic, assist in weight loss, improve your overall health, and essentially turn your body into a fat-burning machine. You can attain all these benefits without worrying about counting calories or making yourself feel deprived of certain foods. Now that you are equipped with all the tools and information you require to make the most of the keto diet, it is time to get started. It is time to let go of the unnecessary fear of fats and embrace them with open arms!

Thank you and all the best!

References

Allen, B. G., Bhatia, S. K., Anderson, C. M., Eichenberger-Gilmore, J. M., Sibenaller, Z. A., Mapuskar, K. A., Schoenfeld, J. D., Buatti, J. M., Spitz, D. R., & Fath, M. A. (2014). Ketogenic diets as an adjuvant cancer therapy: History and potential mechanism. *Redox biology*, *2*, 963–970. https://doi.org/10.1016/j.redox.2014.08.002

Gotter, A. (2018). Keto diet: Benefits and nutrients. Retrieved from https://www.medicalnewstoday.com/articles/31919 6.php#takeaway

Keto Diet Plan for Beginners | Atkins. Retrieved from https://www.atkins.com/how-it-works/library/articles/how-to-start-a-keto-diet-7-tips-for-beginners

Keto Foods – The Ultimate Keto Diet Food List – Key Eats – Heart-First Keto program. Retrieved 14 February 2020, from https://keyeats.com/keto-diet/food-list/

Keto Foods – The Ultimate Keto Diet Food List – Key Eats – Heart-First Keto program. Retrieved from https://keyeats.com/keto-diet/food-list/

Klement, RJ. The emerging role of ketogenic diets in cancer treatment. *Curr Opin Clin Nutr Metab Care.* 2019;22(2):129–134. doi:10.1097/MCO.0000000000000540

Lyon, P. (2019). How To Start A Keto Diet [The Exact Plan To Follow For Beginners]. Retrieved from https://www.ruled.me/how-to-start-a-keto-diet/#how-to-start

Mac, L. (2019). Keto Bodybuilding: Can You Gain Muscle Without Carbs?. Retrieved from https://perfectketo.com/keto-bodybuilding/

Maya. (2018) Low Carb & Keto Diet Plan: How To Start a Low Carb Diet. Retrieved from https://www.wholesomeyum.com/low-carb-keto-diet-plan-how-to-start-a-low-carb-diet/

McMillan, A. (2019). 7 Dangers of Going Keto. Retrieved from https://www.health.com/weight-loss/keto-diet-side-effects

Paoli A, Grimaldi K, Toniolo L, Canato M, Bianco A, Fratter A. Nutrition and acne: therapeutic potential of ketogenic diets. *Skin Pharmacol Physiol*. 2012;25(3):111–117. doi:10.1159/000336404

Rusek M, Pluta R, Ułamek-Kozioł M, Czuczwar SJ. Ketogenic Diet in Alzheimer's Disease. *Int J Mol Sci*. 2019;20(16):3892. Published 2019 Aug 9. doi:10.3390/ijms20163892

Weber, D. D., Aminazdeh-Gohari, S., & Kofler, B. (2018). Ketogenic diet in cancer therapy. *Aging*, *10*(2), 164–165. https://doi.org/10.18632/aging.101382

Made in the USA
Las Vegas, NV
13 October 2024